I0867372

THE NEW ORLEANS JAZZ SCENE

1970–2000

The beloved Doc Cheatham with the author
at a private party in September 1995.

THE New Orleans JAZZ SCENE 1970–2000

A PERSONAL RETROSPECTIVE

THOMAS W. JACOBSEN

Louisiana State University Press *Baton Rouge*

Sea Grant
Louisiana State University

Published with support from the Louisiana Sea Grant College Program, a part of the National Sea Grant College Program maintained by the National Oceanic and Atmospheric Administration of the U.S. Department of Commerce.

Published with the assistance of the Borne Fund

Published by Louisiana State University Press

Manufactured in the United States of America
LSU Press Paperback Original
First printing

Designer: Michelle A. Neustrom
Typeface: Whitman
Printer and binder: Maple Press

Unless otherwise indicated, all photographs are from the author's personal collection.

Library of Congress Cataloging-in-Publication Data

Jacobsen, Thomas W., 1935–, author.
The New Orleans jazz scene, 1970–2000 : a personal retrospective / Thomas W. Jacobsen.
pages cm
"Published with the assistance of the Borne Fund."
Includes bibliographical references and index.
ISBN 978-0-8071-5698-8 (pbk. : alk. paper) — ISBN 978-0-8071-5699-5 (pdf) — ISBN 978-0-8071-5700-8 (epub) — ISBN 978-0-8071-5701-5 (mobi) 1. Jazz—Louisiana—New Orleans—1971–1980—History and criticism. 2. Jazz—Louisiana—New Orleans—1981–1990—History and criticism. 3. Jazz—Louisiana—New Orleans—1991–2000—History and criticism. 4. Jazz musicians—Louisiana—New Orleans. I. Title.
ML3508.8.N48J33 2014
781.6509763'3509045—dc23

2014002831

The paper in this book meets the guidelines for permanence and durability of the Committee on Production Guidelines for Book Longevity of the Council on Library Resources. ♾

To my wife, Sharyn, for her steadfast support throughout this process; and to my daughter Kirsten, for her constant encouragement and thoughtful help in so many different ways.

With thanks and my love always.

CONTENTS

PREFACE

> [New Orleans] is music's epicenter, a cultural ground zero.
>
> —HAROLD BATTISTE, 2010

One may reasonably ask why or how a person who was born and raised at the other end of the Mississippi ends up in New Orleans. Well, you could ask that of a whole lot of people who have come down here. I think, for example, of pianist Butch Thompson, cornetist Charlie DeVore, violinist Matt Rhody, guitarist John Rodli, and clarinetists Brian O'Connell and Chris Kohl. They are all fine musicians, and the city's jazz scene clearly drew them here from the Upper Midwest. (I call the general phenomenon the Lake Wobegon Diaspora. If your taste is in food or music, you come to New Orleans. Otherwise you go to Arizona.) Yet they are but a few of the many who have been attracted to this musical mecca from elsewhere in the States and abroad. In my own case, it was, again, the music as well as the special mystique that makes this city world-famous.

I grew up in a small community—North Mankato—in southern Minnesota. I was born during the Great Depression in 1935, just a few months before the Benny Goodman band made its historic appearance at the Palomar Ballroom in Los Angeles—an event that many have considered the beginning of the Swing Era. My parents were heavily into the big bands and loved to dance to the music of those bands. Neither was a professional musician though my mother had played piano as a teenager for silent movies in the Minnesota village where she grew up. My father was a blue-collar worker who had a nice singing voice—in church. (My mother's intonation was fine, too, but it was always something of an embarrassment to me because she sang too loudly for my taste. My daughter says the same of me.)

Because of my parents' love of the big bands, they often took me as a kid to places like the Orpheum Theater in Minneapolis, where well-known traveling bands and other acts would perform before and after the day's movie attraction. The only band that I can clearly remember seeing in that context was Phil Spitalny and his "all-girl orchestra" featuring "Evelyn and her Magic Violin." I have to say that it did not show me much, but that must have been in the early '40s. Later, once I was hooked on jazz, we would occasionally visit Chicago to see the Cubs play baseball and go to the legendary Blue Note, where I remember seeing the Ellington and Goodman bands. I also remember a special area set aside there for underage kids like myself, where we could drink lemonade or the like and still see and hear the great bands. That was a truly memorable and exciting experience.

The tiny living room of the small three-bedroom bungalow in which I grew up was dominated by a baby grand piano. So it is not surprising that, at the age of five to six, I began taking piano lessons from an elderly lady who lived just a few blocks from our house. (My mother played only "by ear," and she wanted me to get a proper introduction to the instrument.) I continued those lessons and the requisite practicing—grudgingly, preferring to be outside playing ball or almost anything else—until the age of eleven.

At that time, I began taking clarinet lessons from an old German neighbor who was alleged to have played with Sousa. (I have not yet been able to document that association.) Walter Backer was a gruff disciplinarian who had no time for popular music or jazz (which I was beginning to have an interest in), forcing me to work on the classical études. He sat in a chair next to me at our weekly meetings, chewing impatiently on an *unlit* cigar and frequently grabbing my horn out of my hands, saying, "No, no, no, this is the way you must play it"—while leaving bits of cigar residue on my reed and mouthpiece. In spite of all that, I enjoyed playing the clarinet and went through three instruments (from a metal beginner's model, which I wish I would have saved, to a wooden Selmer, which I did save) during the three–four years that I took private lessons from Mr. Backer.

By that time, I was in high school and playing in the marching and concert bands. At the beginning of my junior year (age fifteen, I guess), an opening came up for a tenor saxophone player in what was then called the "swing band" that played for school dances and other special events. Our band director, knowing my proclivities, encouraged me to take up that instrument, which I happily did. My parents had bought all my clarinets up to that point, but I purchased a used Martin tenor for about two hundred dollars with savings from my after-school and summer jobs. I really enjoyed playing the tenor saxophone and, despite taking no formal lessons, picked it up readily because it is a much easier instrument to negotiate than a clarinet. Of course, I continued to play the clarinet as well.

Having grown up before the Television Age (at least in our household), I spent a lot of time listening to the radio—particularly in bed at night, just spinning the dial and seeing what "exotic" stations I could identify. One that I came upon by accident was the "50,000-watt clear-channel voice of New Orleans, WWL" (still 870 on the AM dial), coming in loud and clear at night, even way up in Minnesota. It wasn't long before I heard the Sunday night broadcasts of the New Orleans Jazz Club (NOJC), which had only recently been founded. There were also the live broadcasts from the Blue Room in the Hotel Roosevelt and the Parisian Room on Royal Street, not to overlook the late-night "Moonglow with [Dick] Martin" programs which aired more modern jazz. I was about fourteen at that point and ready for the sounds of traditional New Orleans jazz, with which I could identify much more comfortably than the insipid pop music of the day and the "old time" (polka) music so popular in my part of Minnesota.

Soon I was hooked on the music of New Orleans, especially the clarinetists like Johnny Dodds, Barney Bigard, Jimmy Noone, Irving Fazola, and Pete Fountain—not to mention the bands of Armstrong, Ellington, and a host of others. I was totally enchanted by the theme song of the NOJC broadcasts for most of its life, Johnny Wiggs's blues "Congo Square" with Lester Bouchon on clarinet. I immediately ordered a copy of the record (on 78 rpm, obviously), and have it in my collection to this day. And I am still deeply moved by that haunting melody! It was one of the first in my collection of jazz records that I began assembling at about that time. (The early core of that collection was a few choice 78s from the 1920s in my mother's small collection.) Needless to say, mine has grown to an almost unmanageable size by now.

In my day in that part of the world, junior high school was from seventh through ninth grades. One didn't reach high school until tenth grade. When that happened for me, I met a whole new group of friends, including four or five guys with musical interests similar to my own. One played alto saxophone, another trombone/tuba, and we soon found a piano player, a drummer, and a banjo/baritone sax player. We had a band! One of the guys lived on North Sturgis Street in Mankato, so we called ourselves the "North Sturgis Street Six" and began to get gigs at a variety of local dives and fraternal lodges despite not being members of the musicians' union. (Our high-school band director happened to be president of the local musicians' union and knew about our band, but he kindly overlooked that fact.) We also played on street corners (usually in surrounding villages), wherever there was a chance of getting a few coins as tips. We were pretty good and eventually came in second in a regional NBC radio talent contest won by an Irish tenor who was well known as a former major-league pitcher, Charles "Red" Barrett. (Though out of professional baseball by that time, he still had something of a "name.") He sang a typical Irish melody—I can't remember which one—that persuaded the decision-makers more than our rendition of "Tin Roof Blues." Of course, our parents and friends thought "we was robbed."

The father of one of my bandmates had a large collection of jazz records. It included a lot of Armstrong, Ellington, Beiderbecke, and on and on, as well as a fine Minnesota cornetist by the name of Paul "Doc" Evans (who had New Orleans connections as well). I had an opportunity to hear the Evans band live on numerous occasions and bought most of their recordings from the '40s and '50s. My experience of great music at a fairly early age inspired me to enlarge my own collection. In those days and for some years thereafter, I never really paid much attention to "styles" of jazz, such as New Orleans traditional vs. Dixieland or swing—all were just forms of "jazz." But, when we began reading jazz magazines like *DownBeat*, we learned about "moldy figs," "Dixieland," "boppers," groups that were considered "commercial," and so on. For us, bebop was a new thing and took some getting used to. "Bird" and "Diz" were pretty much the rage among the hippest of the jazz crowd. (There were also the West Coasters who preferred Chet Baker and the Kenton crowd.) But those also just happened to be the years when the "trad revival" was very much alive, and Dixieland, too, was a popular form of jazz.

Those were great years for us because, in the early '50s, nationally known bands were still touring and always made a stop at the large Kato Ballroom across the river in Mankato. Therefore we had opportunities to hear some of the great jazz musicians and bands of that era: Louis Armstrong and his All Stars, the Count Basie Band, Les Brown and his "Band of Renown," Red Nichols and his Five Pennies, to name a few that I can now remember. It was total bliss for us guys because we could stand at the foot of the bandstand and practically reach out and touch those fabulous musicians. And we even had a chance to screw up our courage and speak to some of them. I'll never forget talking to bass saxophonist Joe Rushton (with the Nichols band) and Basie reedman Marshall Royal. In retrospect, I never thought of taking a camera with me to those gigs or even getting autographs. I rather regret that today.[1]

We graduated from high school in 1953, and our band stuck together well into our college years—during the summers, since we all went off in different directions for school. None of us were music majors (though I gave it some thought at one point). We eventually went into a variety of professions: higher education, law, business, and so on. While in college, I sat in once or twice on a local radio program called "A Session for Moldy Figs," playing and talking about some of my own records.

In sum, New Orleans (despite my never having been there) and the NOJC radio broadcasts played a very important part in my early jazz life. Indeed, one of my high-school buddies (the trombonist/attorney/judge) wrote in my senior yearbook that I would probably be running a jazz club in New Orleans one day. And the irony of it is that that almost came to pass in the 1990s when, living down here, I nearly invested in a new jazz venue in the French Quarter! Fortunately, I didn't follow through on it since—like so many music clubs in this city—it went belly up only a few months after it opened.

What eventually brought me to the Crescent City was an opportunity to be a visiting professor at Tulane University in 1988–89. I had made many previous trips to the city since the early 1970s, but they usually were for conferences or speaking engagements and lasted no more than two or three days at a time—though I always managed to catch *some* music while here. The Tulane position presented me with an opportunity to be in the city for almost a full calendar year, allowing me to experience it in all seasons and under many different circumstances. I fell in love with it and vowed to make New Orleans my home in retirement—something that I had been seriously contemplating since the death of my first wife in 1978.[2]

So, I took early retirement from Indiana University in June 1992 and moved here immediately.[3] I took up residence in the Warehouse District ("Arts District") and began to feel like a kid in a candy store! Music nearly every night within easy walking distance from my apartment on Julia Street, and residing right across the street from Emeril's new restaurant. What could have been better? I found the city's laid-back lifestyle very appealing after decades as a hard-working academic. I married my present wife, Sharyn, in 1997.

I soon discovered, however, that New Orleans is not perfect. There are hurricanes, and it can get very hot and humid in the summertime. Crime, corruption, urban blight, and racism are unfortunate facts of life, as is the general social and political conservatism (along with a certain classism) in local society. I was struck, for example, by the pictorial "Social Scene" page in the daily newspaper, not to mention the obsession with football—the Saints and LSU Tigers—nearly to the exclusion of national and international news. Actually, as I was writing this, the owners of the *Times-Picayune* cut back circulation from daily to just three days per week. I have to admit that I do not find that a major disappointment. (I will, however, miss reading the obituaries.) There is a clear disparity in this community, as in so many other places in this country these days, between the haves and have-nots.[4] I should note, however, that, in my experience, the various inequalities here—especially the racial—seem to be worst in the white suburbs and, of course, the outlying regions of the state as a whole.

I was also somewhat surprised and taken aback by the discovery of a keen competitiveness in the music business—not just among the musicians themselves but among the organizations that were purportedly designed to support the musicians and the local jazz scene. I thought that, if those groups worked together rather than at odds with one another, they could stretch the limited resources much farther. The situation caused some organizations, such as the Louisiana Jazz Federation, on whose board I served for a time, simply to fold up their tents and disappear. Although change doesn't happen quickly in this town, I think I may have sensed a slight quickening in that respect over the years since I settled here for good. Another thing that disturbed me was the surprisingly uninformed character of so many in the jazz establishment: community leaders, leaders of organizations dedicated to the support of jazz, and the media (not least, those who wrote about jazz in the local print outlets)—all who trumpeted the importance of the city as the "birthplace of jazz." While all may have known a good deal about Louisiana music in general, many seemed to have only a relatively shallow knowledge of jazz or jazz history, either traditional or modern. Unfortunately, that's the way it is when a newspaper, for example, can afford to hire only one writer to cover the whole of the world of music—and jazz is of serious interest to such a relatively small portion of the total population.[5]

New Orleans is a complex place, though it may not seem so at first glimpse. It is both a cosmopolitan and a multicultural city, but, at the same time, it has many of the qualities of a small town—almost everyone knows everyone else—and is ethnocentric in that it has at times a tendency to overestimate the talents of some of its local artists/entertainers. Yet, while it clearly is not perfect and has many areas that need to be seriously improved, I have never looked back and rarely regretted my decision to move to the Crescent City. In fact, if given the opportunity to relive the whole time, I would have done very little differently. This is a wonderful, unique city, despite the ravages of Hurricane Katrina and the efforts of the tourist industry and developers to homogenize the town. I sincerely believe it has a very promising future. That has been especially apparent to me since Katrina. Very simply, I know of no other place like it in this country. It has become my home and will probably be as long as I am still breathing.

Why, then, this book? Having visited the city over a period of some four decades, lived here (and written about it) for more than two decades, and having been devoted to it and its music for more than a half-century, I felt a need to express my personal thoughts about the New Orleans jazz scene over the period of time with which I was most familiar, from the 1970s to today. I knew of no other book that did so in any detail.

Some years ago I had an opportunity to review Charles Suhor's excellent volume, *Jazz in New Orleans: The Postwar Years through 1970* (2001), for *The Mississippi Rag*. I was very impressed with the manner in which he generally approached the broad subject of jazz, both traditional and modern, in New Orleans over that period of time. (I should also add that I had been very impressed with the reed playing of Charles's older brother, Don. Appreciated among musicians, he was at home in both jazz styles.) Accordingly, when I began to think about the present book, Suhor's study immediately came to mind. I felt that something of a sequel was needed, from 1970 to the present. Therefore I freely admit that Suhor's book was, to a certain extent, the model for mine. I would be delighted if the present effort begins to measure up to its ideal.

But, before turning to the substance of this work, a few words of explanation (or warning?) are probably in order regarding my musical biases and such. We all know that everyone who enjoys music has their favorite players and bands, and I am no different. I suppose mine will become fully apparent in the following though, like Suhor before me, I have tried to give as complete and balanced a picture as possible while realizing full well that it would be impossible to mention every noteworthy individual musician, band, event, or venue. I am quite prepared to listen to those many who will disagree with my judgments or omissions. It is important to remember that, despite my long devotion to jazz, I am not a seriously trained musician. That may be enough to keep some readers from going any further. If so, so be it.

I grew up with traditional jazz, swing, early bop, and "the cool school," but I have come to love and appreciate the later jazz styles as well.[6] It should be understood, however, that jazz has increasingly become more multifaceted with the passage of time and the use of descriptive labels increasingly misleading. I would not consider myself a trad jazz "purist," as some use the term. Nor do I identify with the acronym "OKOM." When I was doing my "New Orleans Notes" column for *The Mississippi Rag*, I received an email from a reader chastising me for straying from "OKOM." I had no clue what that meant, but I soon learned from my editor that it was an acronym for "Our Kind Of Music." I'm still not quite sure what even *that* means. But I gather it refers to traditional jazz in its most limited sense (maybe the jazz of the first two or three decades of the last century and/or the trad revival of later years), and no other jazz style merits attention.

Well, with all due respect to the "OKOMists"—who are certainly entitled to their likes and dislikes, like the rest of us—I tend to see jazz more broadly, as an evolving mainstream (with many tributaries) from its earliest days at the turn of the last century to the present day. I listen to—and like or at least respect—the great bulk of that music, particularly that played by trained musicians. Serious musicians deserve our respect, whether we like their music or not. But I confess to being moved most by those styles in which melody is a critical component and struggle most with the "free" or avant-garde styles. I do not disrespect the latter, and I continue to try (despite my lack of serious training) to appreciate them. Blues and ballads are what I dig most, but they would be followed pretty closely by Afro-Cuban and Brazilian jazz.[7] Beware, too, that I am somewhat partial to instrumental jazz (especially the reed instruments). As for the vocalists, I have a slight preference (always with exceptions) for the females rather than the males. But it is those who are *musicians* as well as singers whom I prefer to listen to.

These are just a few caveats, but my basic philosophy about jazz music is pretty much, as so many of the musicians themselves have put it, "if it swings, I like it." If it seems as if there is a disproportionate emphasis on traditional jazz or Dixieland in what follows, it is merely because that is what this city is most known for—though I hope to demonstrate, as Suhor did so well, that that is not the whole story.

Things have begun to change.

....

This volume is only part of a larger, ongoing study. It focuses on the period of time during which I first began to visit the city (the 1970s) and eventually chose to settle here (the 1990s). Chapter 1 is called a prologue because, in briefly summarizing the scene in New Orleans in the 1960s, it sets the stage for the main body of the work that follows. That begins in chapter 2, an overview of the 1970s from a variety of perspectives beyond simply the musicians and main jazz venues. Thereafter, in chapters 3 and 4, I present a similar look at the 1980s and 1990s respectively, concluding with the year 1999. Chapter 5 is something of a retrospective with concluding thoughts.

While jazz history can never be neatly presented, I have chosen a fairly strict chronological approach—decade by decade. There will be some inevitable overlap, of course. As a former archaeologist (for whom establishing chronological sequences is of primary importance), I felt more comfortable with that approach than, say, a presentation based upon styles or stylistic changes over time. After all, I am a historian rather than a musicologist.

I envision this and perhaps a following volume to be of some use to a fairly broad audience, including specialists and non-specialists alike. The many original photographs in themselves should be of interest to all. They are intended to complement the text and are, like all photographs, unique historical documents. I now regret, however, that my earliest visits to New Orleans were made without camera in tow.

Finally, I would emphasize that the following is a rather personalized account of the subject matter. The reader will doubtless notice more use of the first-person than the third-person passive constructions so often seen in scholarly writing. The emphasis, after all, is upon the period in New Orleans jazz history that I have been most directly connected with. My reactions and experiences are, accordingly, purely my own. Others might well see things quite differently.

I can only hope that all readers will find something in this volume of interest. May the reading be an enjoyable experience for all.

ACKNOWLEDGMENTS

It is impossible to thank all who have helped and inspired me during my years in New Orleans. This is a city where it is so easy to meet people (even for me), and I am extremely grateful for the many good friends that I gained during the past two decades or more here. I can only apologize to those whom I have overlooked in the following paragraphs.

I would like to begin by expressing my most sincere gratitude to those who have taken time to read portions of my manuscript prior to publication and have provided valuable feedback. The list includes Eddie Bayard, John Doheny, Andrea DuPlessis, John Mahoney, Don Marquis, Steve Masakowski, Royal Stokes, and Charlie Suhor. I would also like to thank the anonymous outside reviewer of my manuscript for his encouraging words and suggestions.

Beyond those, I would like to express my thanks to the following for their thoughts and kind help along the way: Lynn Abbott, the late Dick Allen, Bengt Andersson, Deano Assunto, Al Belletto, David Boeddinghaus, Jerry Brock, Charles Chamberlain, Sandra Dartus, the late George Finola, Pete Fountain, Danny Gamble, Banu Gibson, Matt Goldman, Lee Goode, Mike Gourrier, Matt Hassebrock, Joseph Hebert, Duke Heitger, George Hocutt, Connie Jones, Edward "Kidd" Jordan, Fred Laredo, Tom McDermott, Ray Moore, Jason Patterson, Michael Pellera, Donna Poniatowski, Bruce Raeburn, Trevor Richards, Will Severns, John "Kid" Simmons, Rhodes Spedale, the late Richard "Dickie" Taylor, Ian Thiele, Chris Tyle, Don Vappie, Dr. Michael White, and Clive Wilson.

I would also like to acknowledge with gratitude the New Orleans Jazz and Heritage Foundation for awarding me a 2012 Community Partnership Grant for archive documentation (ADM12-105). It has helped immensely in the preparation of this book.

Finally, I would like to note how much I learned from the wonderful conversations that I had with the splendid New Orleans musicians (led by the incomparable Lionel Ferbos who turned 102 in 2013) whom I interviewed for my book *Traditional New Orleans Jazz* (2011). The reader will see that I refer extensively to those conversations in this volume as well.

THE NEW ORLEANS JAZZ SCENE
1970–2000

1

Prologue

THE 1960S

"Beatlemania" dominated the national music scene in the 1960s.[1] While jazz continued to evolve from the rather dramatic and exciting developments of the late 1940s and 1950s, the popularity of the Beatles and other rock groups doubtless led to a decline in audience numbers on the national level—especially among younger listeners. With giants such as Miles, Coltrane, Bill Evans, Stan Getz, and Buddy DeFranco—to pick just five personal favorites—performing at high levels, the decline can hardly be due to a lack of available jazz talent. The earlier Dixieland and trad craze also seems to have begun to wane at the national level.

Was the New Orleans jazz scene similarly affected? Some observers have suggested that such was the case.

A few visitors found reasons to complain about what they found here. The well-known German jazz historian and critic, the late Joachim E. Berendt, and famed American jazz photographer, the late William Claxton, made a joint cross-country trip in the United States in 1960 that ultimately led to a book, originally published in Germany.[2] Their journey included a nine-day sojourn in New Orleans, after which they observed, "'You don't even need to bother to go to New Orleans. Jazz in New Orleans is dead,' they told us in New York. We heard the same thing again in Biloxi, Miss.—and Biloxi is barely 30 miles from New Orleans." Berendt and Claxton went on to observe, "Even before you get to New Orleans, you can already tell from the roadside billboards that on Bourbon Street—the so-called 'main street of jazz' in New Orleans—jazz is commercialized." They later added, "many people say jazz in New Orleans is dead because they think of Bourbon Street. Bourbon Street, in the old French Quarter, has long been regarded as the main street of jazz life in New Orleans. But when you get there you find very little jazz, and a solid half of what little is there is questionable.

"On the other hand," they go on, "there are that many more striptease shows. I [presumably Berendt] counted 20 striptease clubs and five jazz clubs on Bourbon Street. The ratio is improved by the fact that, in many of the striptease clubs, second-rate jazz is played as background music as the girls undress."[3]

Such are the comments of two outsiders whose stay in the city was certainly brief. They are, at least in part, value judgments. What do the authors (presumably Berendt for the most part) mean by "jazz," especially when they judge it to be "second-rate"? Nor is attention given to the emerging contemporary jazz scene in the city at the time. The story also accentuates the brevity of their visit by a number of errors of fact. Nevertheless, it represents a view of jazz in the city that was by no means unique at the time.

Another outsider, NBC television news icon David Brinkley, paid a visit to New Orleans in 1962. He noted in his ensuing coverage that strip clubs "are taking over for" jazz clubs on Bourbon Street.[4]

This raised the hackles of a number of locals in the media, including Charles Suhor, who writes,

> [*DownBeat* editor] Don De Michael printed my March 15, 1962, news story on the NBC-TV *David Brinkley's Journal* coverage of the Hall [Preservation Hall] and the local jazz scene. New Orleans *States-Item* columnist Bob Sublette had rightly panned the TV story's a priori assertion that jazz was being "replaced" by strippers—the exact opposite of what was developing as a result of [Pete] Fountain and [Al] Hirt's local engagements after winning national fame. Glad to see some local copy devoted to jazz, I fanned the flames by supporting Sublette locally and doing the *DB* news story. Later that year I submitted the full-length article on the Hall—the first, I believe, in a national journal.[5]

This little dustup in the early 1960s is reminiscent of the never-ending concerns over the commercialization of Bourbon Street, the main street of tourism in the city. Today, it is the ubiquitous T-shirt shops that have locals—and most everyone else of sound mind—incensed about "The Street." And a familiar refrain among those visitors (especially those who have traveled from abroad) to "the birthplace of jazz" in the years I have been living here is, "where is the jazz"? Well, it's still there to some degree, but, as I tell them, one must look beyond Bourbon Street as well. Yet more about all of that later. Suffice it to say for the present that the local authorities, led by then–District Attorney Jim Garrison, soon initiated a crackdown on the strip-club scene.[6] It has not been stamped out altogether, however.

To return to our brief overview of the scene in New Orleans in the '60s, I must defer to Suhor, the insider, once again. In 1966, he argued strongly that the city was, in fact, "ready for its New Golden Age,"[7] as he demonstrated by stressing the importance of Preservation Hall, which opened for business in 1961. Beyond that, in the traditional realm, he points to Pete Fountain and Al Hirt returning to town and opening their own clubs on The Street.

In addition to the veteran players and bands (for example, trombonist Santo Pecora [1902–1984] at the Famous Door on Bourbon Street), the decade is marked by the arrival of a number of talented youngsters who eventually came to make names for themselves in traditional jazz in the city and internationally.

The idea behind Preservation Hall (PH) was to give older, largely African American jazz musicians work and thereby keep the city's traditional music alive. "There is no question that Preservation Hall saved New Orleans jazz," says impresario George Wein, founder of the New Orleans Jazz & Heritage Festival and the famed Newport Jazz Festival. "When it became an institution in New Orleans, everybody who went down there went to the hall. They paid a dollar [the entrance fee is now twelve dollars] to go hear people like George Lewis [1900–1968] or Sweet Emma Barrett [1897–1983] and made them national figures."[8]

It should perhaps be noted that the success of Preservation Hall spawned a number of imitators/clones who had varying degrees of success. None lasted very long. Perhaps the most successful was Dixieland Hall, which started out in 1962 at 516 Bourbon Street and featured the music of the Louis Cottrell band. But it did not last beyond the mid-1970s. Another was Economy Hall in the Royal Sonesta Hotel on Bourbon Street. It also served as a temporary home of the New Orleans Jazz

Club's collection in the late '60s before the assemblage moved on to another temporary home in the 800 block of Conti Street in the 1970s. Heritage Hall was yet another. Southland Hall, across the street from Preservation Hall, was still another. But none of the imitators managed to outlive their model.

In 1963, Preservation Hall owner and tubist Allan Jaffe (1935–1987) formed the hall's first traveling band, which as Tom Sancton notes, "turned Preservation Hall into a lucrative operation. . . . The tours eventually took the P.H.J.B. as far as Moscow and Tokyo, and they remain a big part of the operation today."[9]

The concerts of those traveling bands (including the likes of the revered and oft-imitated clarinetist George Lewis) were seen and heard by many throughout the world and doubtless enticed a host of young players in foreign countries to visit New Orleans. Among those who arrived from abroad in the early to mid-1960s were multi-instrumentalist Lars Edegran and clarinetist Orjan "Orange" Kellin from Sweden; drummer Barry Martyn, reedman Sammy Rimington, drummer Trevor Richards, trumpeters John "Kid" Simmons and Clive Wilson, all from the U.K.; trumpeter Yoshio and his wife, pianist/banjoist Keiko, Toyama from Japan; and the list goes on and on.[10]

There were a number of Americans who came to the city and lived here for a while as well. Of those who did not stay permanently, most return frequently for visits. Trumpeter Charlie Devore and pianist/clarinetist Butch Thompson, for example, came from the upper Midwest (Minnesota/Wisconsin) early on. A twenty-year-old cornetist from Chicago, via Nashville, created quite a stir (both locally and nationally) in the mid-sixties with a recording he made with some of the city's veteran all-stars. George Finola (1945–2000), while raised on Bix and the so-called Chicago style, "chose our city because of its great musical history and because New Orleans is a place where jazz musicians congregate and can make a living playing their music. Jazz is still the music of the city."[11] Finola's album, *Jazz of the Chosen Few* (1965), was recorded live at the original Jazz Museum on Dumaine Street. It included guitarist Danny Barker (1909–1994) and his vocalist wife, Blue Lu (1913–1998). The Barkers had just returned to the city from a thirty-year "sabbatical" in New York City.

The year 1961 is noteworthy for another reason. The New Orleans Jazz Club's museum—said to be the world's first jazz museum—opened at its original location on Dumaine Street in the French Quarter during that year. The core of the collection was memorabilia assembled by banjoist-guitarist Dr. Edmond "Doc" Souchon (1897–1968), but the real attractions of the collection came to be the many musical instruments associated with a host of New Orleans jazz greats (including Louis Armstrong). As it happened, Finola and Danny Barker served as curators for a brief time at the outset. The itinerant NOJC collection then moved to Economy Hall in the Royal Sonesta Hotel in 1969 and still later to a location on Conti Street (across the street from today's Prince Conti Hotel) in the French Quarter. Eventually, it was turned over to the Louisiana State Museum (Old U.S. Mint) on Esplanade Avenue in 1977, where it was often referred to simply as the "Jazz Museum." Yet it was not until October 1983 that the NOJC collection was officially opened to the public.[12]

The Dukes of Dixieland, led by the New Orleanian Assunto brothers —trumpeter Frank (1932–1974) and trombonist Freddie (1929–1966)— maintained the national popularity that they had achieved with their many recordings and appearances on the Ed Sullivan television show in the late 1950s.[13] But, it seems, they spent more time in Las Vegas than in New Orleans in the 1960s. While the band was usually dismissed by the purists as too "commercial," clarinetist Jack Maheu, who played and recorded with the Dukes for a couple of years in the later '50s, does not entirely agree. "Freddie and Frankie were good players," he recalls. "And that band, when it was on, it sounded good—good jazz—and got across, people loved it. There just wasn't enough diversity for me."[14]

The only New Orleanians acknowledged in the critics' or readers' polls during the decade were, of course, Louis Armstrong (1901–1971), both as trumpeter and singer (multiple times); Pete Fountain, several times in the clarinet category; and trumpeter Al Hirt (1922–1999), just once as an instrumentalist.[15] Armstrong's hit "Hello Dolly" reached number one on the popularity charts, making him the oldest person at the time to achieve that distinction. The purists, of course, also charged him with "going commercial," and even his excellent band—the All Stars— was often dismissed by them for the same reasons.[16]

Legendary trombonist Jack Teagarden (1905–1964), a member of Armstrong's original All Stars, left that group in the early 1950s and started his own sextet, which ultimately included New Orleans cornetist Conrad "Connie" Jones, another excellent young horn player in the city at that time. Ironically, Teagarden, whose health had been declining, died of pneumonia in New Orleans in January 1964. (Accordingly, a plaque commemorating his death can be seen today outside the Seaport Café and Bar in the 400-block of Bourbon Street.) Jones was living in the Philadelphia area while traveling with "Big T" and moved back there for a year or so with his family after Teagarden's death. But he was called back to his hometown by Pete Fountain in 1966 and has retained the city as his base since that time. He has achieved a distinguished career as a highly respected bandleader and featured soloist.[17]

A surprising number of modernists have grown up in New Orleans, the world capital of traditional jazz. Some headed elsewhere—as is often the case—for broader exposure, but many of them (like many traditionalists) either stayed at home or came back after moving away. Some of them are still around, too. The list would include bassists Peter "Chuck" Badie and Richard Payne (1931–2001); drummers Tony "Oulabula" Bazley, Ed Blackwell (1929–1992), and James Black (1940–1988); saxophonists Al Belletto, Harold Battiste, and Alvin "Red" Tyler (1925–1998); clarinetist Alvin Batiste (1932–2007); clarinetist and saxophonist Don Suhor (1932–2003), older brother of Charles; guitarist and bassist Bill Huntington; and pianist Ellis Marsalis Jr.

Some of those names may even be better known now in the traditional field. That is, in fact, a characteristic of New Orleans musicians. They can (or must) move quite comfortably from one jazz style to another (not to mention R&B as well). Drummer Ernie Elly recalled recently, "I remember one day I played about four gigs and each gig was a different type of music. I was proud of that, you know."[18] Needless to say, that phenomenon is also due in part to the exigencies of work opportunities. As local reedman John Doheny put it, "New Orleans musicians—and South Louisiana musicians—have a very large stylistic palette in their repertoire. You can find jazz musicians all over who know a lot of *jazz* tunes, but they tend to be out of their depth once you leave that genre.

Professional players here, older cats in particular but many of the young players as well, simply know a ridiculous amount of material. They have to, in order to make a living."[19] It has never been easy to be a modernist in this city, but I am happy to say that the situation has been gradually improving over recent decades.

One of the most widely known modernists in the '60s from New Orleans was alto saxophonist Al Belletto, who had gained national recognition in the '50s for his recordings on the Capitol label under the auspices of bandleader Stan Kenton. He returned home in 1961 to become musical director of the new Playboy Club, 721 Iberville Street (between Royal and Bourbon), where he hired a variety of other top contemporary musicians. Suhor calls this club "a major force in the growth of modern jazz in New Orleans."[20]

Belletto opened eight other Playboy Clubs across the country and trained most of the musical directors of those clubs. He was, in fact, responsible for the hiring of the fine Danish-born trombonist Kai Winding to direct the musical activities at the well-known club in New York City.[21]

Racial segregation in the early part of the decade presented problems in hiring musicians. As Carolyn Kolb reported, "Belletto, even under those limitations, was able to hire black musicians (including pianist Ellis Marsalis), and ultimately Belletto's own band at the club was integrated."[22] Marsalis adds, "I did like it. The instrument [i.e., the piano] was good, it was good money at the time, and I had a chance to work out quite a few things in a trio format. We played downstairs, and then we backed up black performers that came in." By the time he worked there again later, however, the law had changed.[23]

Another significant project in the modern idiom was the four-LP boxed anthology put together by New Orleans saxophonist Harold Battiste: *New Orleans Heritage: Jazz 1956–1966* on the Opus 43 label. It was the product of a local African American musical experiment known as "All for One" (AFO) formed by Battiste. The anthology features early recordings by some of those modern pathfinders in the city, including Battiste himself, along with others who ultimately gained national reputations: pianist Ellis Marsalis, drummers Blackwell and Black, clarinetist Alvin Batiste, and cornetist Melvin Lastie (1930–1972), to name only a few.

Harold Battiste was an extremely important figure on the modern jazz scene in New Orleans, though not always widely recognized as such on a national level. A graduate of Dillard University in the city, he was an arranger and producer as well as a practicing musician. He moved to Los Angeles in 1963, where he became well known for his work in the film, television, and recording industries. He was associated, very successfully indeed, with Sonny and Cher for some fifteen years. He returned to New Orleans in 1989 to join Ellis Marsalis in starting the jazz studies program at the University of New Orleans, from which he has since retired.[24] He celebrated his eightieth birthday in 2011.

Jazz festivals emerged seriously in this country in the mid-1950s.[25] In fact, the first one took place in Newport, Rhode Island, in 1954. Pianist and jazz-club owner George Wein was hired to organize it. That festival has had a memorable, though somewhat checkered, history to the present day.

New Orleans joined the jazz-festival circuit essentially for the first time in 1968. (Al Belletto later noted that he was one of the co-founders of that event.) The eight-day fest featured many local bands complemented by an impressive array of out-of-town talent that included the Duke Ellington band, Dave Brubeck, Gerry Mulligan, Ramsey Lewis, and traditionalists Max Kaminsky, Art Hodes, and Pee Wee Russell. The event was such a success that plans were quickly made for a repeat in the following year. The 1969 edition, however, seems to have been more successful artistically than commercially.[26] Those two events served as the foundation upon which the "official" New Orleans Jazz and Heritage Festival began, under Wein's guidance, in 1970.

The decade of the '60s was a time of racial unrest, not least in the South. While the Civil Rights Act of 1964 was of epic importance, it clearly did not solve all the problems of racism in Louisiana. Yet New Orleans has a fairly long history of informal or sub-rosa racial interaction among performing musicians, despite the state's 1956 law against "interracial entertainments."[27]

Because of segregation, there had been two—one black, the other white—musicians' unions in New Orleans until they merged in 1969, the year after Dr. Martin Luther King's assassination. It is interesting that many of the foreign musicians who came to the city in the mid-sixties chose to join the black, rather than the white, union.[28]

To sum up, the most influential (long-term) jazz accomplishments of the decade of the 1960s were, not necessarily in any order of priority: (1) The foundation of Preservation Hall. (2) The establishment of the Jazz Museum. (3) The planting of the seeds of the New Orleans Jazz and Heritage Festival and, by extension, the many other festivals featuring jazz that eventually came to characterize the city. (4) The recognition of New Orleans as an incubator for modern (as well as traditional) jazz musicians. Contrary to the reports of some visitors and what may have been happening on the national level, New Orleans had a lively jazz scene during this decade. That may be, in fact, another indication of the city's conservative nature.

In addition, two of the most severe hurricanes in the area's history, prior to the devastating Katrina-Rita tandem, took place in the last half of this decade: Hurricane Betsy (1965), a Category 3 storm that became the first billion-dollar hurricane in the United States, and Hurricane Camille (1969), a Category 5 that was the third deadliest in the twentieth century in this country. Insofar as I can determine, the effects of these disasters were relatively short-lived from the point of view of the local jazz scene. They certainly did not approach the devastation wrought by the flooding of Katrina, with its manifold implications for the local music community.

Preservation Hall today looks pretty much as it did in the 1960s.

Preservation Hall Jazz Band, late 1960s or early 1970s. *Left to right:* Louis Nelson, trombone; Chester Jones, drums; George "Kid Sheik" Colar, trumpet; Sylvester Handy, bass; Raymond Burke, clarinet; Charlie Hamilton, piano; Emanuel Sayles, banjo. *Photograph courtesy of Preservation Hall.*

Saxophonist Al Belletto was one of the pioneer modernists in New Orleans. He is seen here in a 1980s JazzFest performance with two of his longtime sidemen, bassist Bill Huntington and drummer Johnny Vidacovich.

Connie Jones was one of the young lions in the 1960s and remains a much-admired trumpeter today.

The original New Orleans Jazz Museum at 1017 Dumaine Street, ca. 1965. This photograph was taken by Terry Friedman and is on display at the Jazz Museum in the Old Mint.

George Finola (with cornet, *center right*) at the French Quarter Festival, 1980s. Finola was one of the talented "imports" to the New Orleans jazz scene in the 1960s and became an instant success. He is joined here by trombonist Paul Crawford, clarinetist Jacques Gauthé, sousaphonist Tom Saunders, and Neil Unterseher on banjo. The drummer is unidentified.

Saxophonist Harold Battiste was one of the pioneers of modern jazz in the city, having founded All for One Records in the early 1960s. Later, after a lengthy stay on the West Coast, he returned to become one of the charter faculty members of the jazz studies program at the University of New Orleans.

Pete Fountain, a New Orleans legend, returned to the city after a two-year stint on the popular Lawrence Welk TV show in the late 1950s and founded his first club on Bourbon Street. Fountain is probably the most beloved jazz musician in the city today, as is indicated by the enthusiastic reception he received at French Quarter Fest in 2008.

George Wein at the piano at JazzFest. The "father" of jazz festivals in this country, he founded the Newport Jazz Festival in the 1950s and later the "official" New Orleans Jazz and Heritage Festival.

The late Al "Jumbo" Hirt is a New Orleans legend. He was at his peak in the mid-1960s, when he was considered one of the top trumpeters in the country. He also ran a popular jazz club on Bourbon Street for many years.

2

Jazz Is Back

THE 1970S

The decade of the '70s opened in New Orleans with Maurice "Moon" Landrieu assuming the office of mayor of the city. He had been a staunch (and virtually unique) supporter of equal rights during his time in the state legislature. As mayor he called the new decade a time of hope, probably in large part because Louisiana's economy was flourishing due to high energy prices. As it turned out, he was the last white mayor of New Orleans until his son, Mitch, was elected to the office in 2011.

Landrieu was succeeded by Ernest "Dutch" Morial in 1978, who became the first African American mayor of the city. (His son, Marc, also served as mayor from 1994 to 2002.) Both mayors Landrieu and Morial realized the importance of tourism to the city's economy and did a great deal to attract visitors to New Orleans. The popular promenade called the "Moonwalk," which stretches along the Mississippi in the French Quarter, was a product of the first Landrieu administration. The convention center, now known as the Ernest N. Morial Convention Center, was begun during that mayor's administration. It has continued to expand in size since that time. The first Super Bowl was held in Tulane University's stadium (the old Sugar Bowl stadium as well) in 1970, and the Louisiana Superdome opened in 1975, bringing more hotels to the Central Business District. Needless to say, the promise of expanded tourism coupled with increased convention business could have been expected to bring more work for local musicians. In fact, looking back on the decade, one local musician considered the '70s as something of a "golden age" for himself—what with the convention gigs and the appearance of the "jazz brunch" (first at Commander's Palace, an upscale Uptown restaurant).[1]

On the national jazz scene, there seems to have been an increase in the jazz audience. Upon the opening of the decade, the distinguished jazz historian and critic Dan Morgenstern observed, "As we enter the

'70s, interest in jazz among young Americans is once again on the upswing, and by mid-decade there is another jazz recording boom."[2]

An article in *Newsweek* in the same year expands on that observation:

> All of a sudden, *le jazz* is hot. Pushed into a neutral corner by rock in the '60s, jazz has at last come out fighting. The signs of rebirth are everywhere, from Chicago's avant-garde and New York's Bohemian lofts to the hundreds of Dixieland lovers in New Orleans who follow the French Market Jazz Band that marches through the streets of the French Quarter. Attendance at this summer's Newport Jazz Festival in New York . . . broke all records. And the sale of record albums, new and old, would make a pop star weep. There are jazz cruises, jazz museums and jazz colleges.
>
> Ten years ago in New York there were fewer than ten jazz clubs. Today there are 80. Seven years ago in Boston there was just one. Now there are 21. Their number has doubled in Los Angeles in the last three years, and on Chicago's Lincoln Avenue it's reaching the proportions of an epidemic. . . . Jazz not only has a past but it has a future again.[3]

The *Newsweek* piece pays much attention to the advent of what was called "jazz-fusion" or "jazz-rock," clearly an attempt to do something different, to popularize jazz, but—more so, in my opinion—an experiment to get young people involved in the jazz scene once again and thereby expand the audience. Electronics and amplification began to play a role in jazz like never before. I have to say, however, that Miles Davis's album *Bitch's Brew*—despite its enormous popularity—did not do for me what his marvelous *Kind of Blue* album had done a decade earlier. In any case, by the end of the decade, jazz-fusion had pretty much run its course in popularity (though by no means did it disappear).

Other jazz styles (such as the free jazz of Ornette Coleman, who had spent some time in New Orleans in the 1950s) continued to be appealing to some and may even have increased in appeal. From my experience in Greece during those years (and thereafter), free jazz—or, as some Europeans called it, "improvisational music"—seems to have been even more popular on that continent (and in Germany in particular) and continued to be so into the '80s and beyond.

There was something of a resurgence of the big bands in this country as well. The fine orchestras of jazz titans such as Count Basie, Duke Ellington, Woody Herman, and Stan Kenton were still doing well. Unfortunately, two of my all-time favorite big-band leaders—Ellington (1974) and Kenton (1979)—were lost to us during the decade. Yet a wonderful new band led by Japanese-Chinese pianist, composer, and arranger Toshiko Akiyoshi, hit the charts at that time. A featured soloist for the band was her husband, the fine tenor saxophonist and flutist Lew Tabackin. The band had many other first-rate sidemen, and they became a big hit with jazz fans and big-band lovers like myself. For a time, I bought every one of their many albums as each was released.

So it was on the national level. Let's see to what extent New Orleans, rarely a national pace-setter after the early years, mirrors that national scene.

THE PASSING OF LOUIS ARMSTRONG

Another giant that passed during the decade was, of course, New Orleans's own Louis Armstrong (June 6, 1971). He died and was buried in New York City, where he had lived for many years. "Armstrong's death was front-page news around the world . . . [His] body was laid out for three days at the New York National Guard Armory for the more than twenty-five thousand fans who went to say good-bye."[4] While musicians came from near and far (including New Orleans) to pay final tribute to "Pops," the ceremony seems to have been a very somber occasion—not what a New Orleanian might expect. There was no music at all, a sad fact that astonished most in the jazz world.[5]

Such was *not* the case in Armstrong's hometown, where fifteen thousand worshippers turned out for a memorial tribute in front of City Hall less than a week after his death—June 11, 1971. It was an appropriate location for the ceremony since it was held in the neighborhood in which the great trumpeter had been born. Unfortunately, a gigantic miscalculation by the city fathers had destroyed the Armstrong home on (the former) Jane Alley in the late 1950s—a horrendous tragedy that we continue to rue to this day and will never live down among jazz fans the world over.

Charles Suhor's account of the occasion in *DownBeat* (1972) opens with the following words: "No one expected that more than 10,000 persons would show up for the Louis Armstrong memorial services in New Orleans five days after his death. So the hubbub and confusion that resulted couldn't be blamed on the planners—mostly New Orleans Jazz Club members—who were prepared for neither the size nor the mood of the crowd.

"As I got out of my car at O'Keefe Avenue," Suhor continues, "I felt a brisk air of anticipation in the steady stream of people walking toward Duncan Plaza near City Hall. *My God,* I thought, *do all these people love Louis? Do they know that he was not just a celebrity but a great artist and genius of our time?*"[6]

The ceremony took place, but not without some glitches. It opened with a couple of tunes by the young Fairview Baptist Church band recently organized by Danny Barker.[7] The more traditional Olympia and Onward brass bands were also to have performed, but they were unable to penetrate the huge crowd and had to remain on the periphery. There were the expected speeches by the mayor, clergymen, and Dick Allen of the Tulane Jazz Archive. The solemnities concluded with Teddy Riley performing "Taps" on the cornet on which Armstrong first learned to play at the Colored Waif's Home in 1913. The horn, which was originally purchased by George Finola and lent to the NOJC's jazz collection, where it stayed until returned to him in the 1990s, was reacquired by the museum after Finola's death in 2000. It is now on prominent display as one enters the renovated exhibit in the Louisiana State Museum (the Old U.S. Mint).

Then the crowd took over. As Suhor put it, "In New Orleans a crowd doesn't gather just to *see* something. A crowd rapidly becomes something in itself—something for dancing, for marching, or just milling around being a crowd. . . . New Orleans is a Third World sort of environment where the people cannot be relied upon to act reverential, progressive, conservative, chic, civic-minded, or anything else in the way that Americans usually think of these terms."[8] In short, the contrast between the way the two memorials were carried out in New York City and in New Orleans is quite striking, highlighting the uniqueness of the Crescent City.

Further recognition was in store for Armstrong in his real hometown, but, as often in this city, it did not come quickly—or exactly as envisioned. Already in 1969 California-based jazz enthusiast and writer Floyd Levin (1922–2007), inspired by an offhand comment by Danny Barker (1909–1994), hatched a plan for an Armstrong statue. He organized a "Hello Louis" fund-raiser in his hometown of Los Angeles in 1970—on what was then thought to be Louis's seventieth birthday[9]—at which a number of New Orleans musicians performed. Thus the project was underway, and the highly respected artist Elizabeth Catlett (then living in Mexico City) was commissioned to do the $30,000 greater-than-life-size sculpture.[10]

In 1972, there was a public announcement revealing the plan to create a fifty-acre "Louis Armstrong Memorial Park" along North Rampart Street in the Tremé neighborhood, adjacent to the French Quarter. Despite much controversy and delay, the park was officially opened by Mayor Landrieu on July 4, 1976—the nation's bicentennial.

The plan also called for the dedication of the Armstrong sculpture in the new park at the same time, but the necessary funding for the completion of the monument was slow to come in despite Levin's tireless efforts. Finally, with the help of an eleventh-hour contribution by singer Bing Crosby, the completed statue reached New Orleans—but *not Armstrong Park*—by July 4, 1976. Instead, the dedication ceremony took place in Jackson Square in the center of the French Quarter—on the U.S. Bicentennial and what was thought to be Armstrong's seventy-sixth birthday. Danny Barker's Jazz Hounds were on hand to play "Happy Birthday, Dear Satchmo," and Blue Lu Barker (1914–1998) sang it. A big crowd had gathered for the ceremony, and they were entertained by Albert "Papa" French (1910–1977) and his Original Tuxedo Jazz Band. It was a joyous occasion. We are told that some fifteen hundred jazz fans from around the world had contributed to the statue fund.[11]

Eventually, the statue reached its proper resting place in Armstrong Park, but the story was still not complete. The park experienced severe damage from Hurricane Katrina, and the statue itself was further damaged by a klutzy repair crew contracted by then-Mayor Ray Nagin thereafter. As of this writing, the embarrassment has finally been rectified.

A SELECTION OF NEW ORLEANS LIVE JAZZ VENUES IN THE 1970S

The following is based in part on a frank but somewhat cynical account of one local jazz aficionado and writer, Harlan Wood, who had moved to New Orleans from New York City and was asked by editor Don Marquis to give his impressions of the local scene for *The Second Line* magazine.[12]

Wood opens his piece with the following words: "Much has been written in the past few years that jazz in New Orleans is in perpetual decline. Partly, this is true; partly, it is false. Good and great jazz still exists in the Crescent City—but, in the Quarter today you have to search it out." That was the main point of his article. While he is not so specific—in terms of relative numbers—as in the *Newsweek* article cited above, Wood does at least present a reasonable sample of what clubs existed in the French Quarter in mid-decade and who played at them. It makes some sense in light of my own experience from several visits to the city during different times in the seventies. Let us begin by looking at the clubs in the French Quarter.

Not mentioned by Wood, the **Playboy Club** was located at 727 Iberville Street. It was already a well-established modern jazz venue in the '60s because saxophonist Al Belletto and his group were the house band. Indeed, Belletto hired all the music at the club. As near as can be determined now (with the kind help of Belletto himself), his ensemble performed there until the venue closed in 1974. Al was known as "coach" to the younger members of his group. They recorded an LP in 1973 called "Coach's Choice" that featured the regulars who played with him in the club: Bill Huntington, bass; Johnny Vidacovich, drums; Frank Puzzullo, piano; and vocalists Angelle Trosclair, Linda Aubert, and Edie Aikels. Both Huntington and Puzzullo taught in the jazz studies program at Loyola University, while Vidacovich, now a legend in the city, was just a twenty-four-year-old kid at the time.[13]

There were several rooms with music at the club: upstairs, downstairs, the Library, and the VIP Playhouse. "The gig was really good," says Vidacovich, whose uncle was the fine but oft-overlooked trad clarinetist Irvine "Pinky" Vidacovich (1905–1966). "When I first came to work we'd play a set downstairs, jazz. Then you'd go upstairs for a show. Then you'd have another show."[14]

On Iberville near Bourbon was the **Gateway Lounge**, where Neil Unterseher and his Razzberrie Ragtimers performed. Unterseher is a veteran banjoist (and practicing artist) who still plays around town. Wood suggested that they could "play solid [traditional] jazz if you ask."

Wood calls **Pete Fountain**'s club at 231 Bourbon Street "one helluva place," in part because of the presence of legendary reedman Eddie Miller (1911–1991), who was one of the members of the house band. Miller was a fine clarinetist, too, but he played mainly tenor sax (and very well, I might add) in Pete's ensemble. He was one of those musicians (like Lester Young, Jimmy Giuffre, and a handful of others) known mostly as tenor players but who were more than competent clarinet players as well. But, of course, it was Fountain himself, with his national reputation, that drew the tourists and packed the house regularly.

A visitor during that era also had to check out **Al Hirt**'s Bourbon Street club. It was there that I was introduced to Hirt's clarinetist, Joseph "PeeWee" Spitelera (1937–1985), whom I heard live for the first time. He was one of the many fine New Orleans musicians who did not receive the kind of wider attention they deserved, probably because he stayed close to home most of his life. But, again, it was "Jumbo" himself who drew the crowds.

The **Esplanade Café**, at the corner of Bourbon and Toulouse, offered live jazz only intermittently. "When it's there, it is basically good," Wood writes, noting that when trumpeter/cornetist Connie Jones is on hand "it's worth it." Jones, a native New Orleanian, is yet another local musician who may not have received the kind of national and international attention he so richly deserves. I cannot count how many fellow musicians have spoken in reverent tones about his creative ideas, tasteful improvisation, and mastery of his instrument. He is one of a kind.

The **Blue Angel**, just a few doors away from Fountain's, was the only club that I visited on *each* of my trips to the city during the decade. The afternoon band there was led either by very able trumpeters Murphy Campo (1935–1993) or Jimmy Ille (1921–1999). But it was the night band led by young cornetist George Finola, whose debut recording had made such a good impression on me, that attracted me most. He always had good sidemen with him, including trombonists such as the very talented Paul Crawford (1925–1996) or (like Spitelera) the underrated Tom Geckler (who retired in 1995); Phamous Lambert (1930–2000) on piano; and, again, the under-appreciated Clarence Ford (1929–1994) on clarinet. The latter was also a very good saxophonist (both alto and tenor). His son Louis, also a reed player, has maintained the family tradition of excellence today.

Finola, who grew up in Chicago, was influenced by Bix, but, somewhat surprisingly, so were a couple of native New Orleanian horn players: the wonderful Johnny Wiggs (1899–1977) and the short-lived pioneer Emmett Hardy (1903–1925). Of course none of the three pretended to be Bix clones, but, as a Beiderbecke admirer from my youth, I could identify well with the playing of both Finola and Wiggs. On one of my visits during the decade (1977), I made it a point to bring my son Mark, who was then a cornetist in his middle-school band, just to hear Finola, and the latter was kindly encouraging (despite his somewhat cantankerous reputation). Wood has this to say about the club: "The Blue Angel has adopted the strip-joint pricing policy and the music is too good to need this—it keeps New Orleanians away." Nonetheless, Finola managed to play a record twelve consecutive years at the Blue Angel, he later told me.[15]

The **Paddock Lounge**, a first-rate jazz club through the years, featured the fine trumpeter Wallace Davenport (1925–2004) at times. Davenport, a New Orleans native, had a good deal of big-band experience (with the likes of Lionel Hampton and Count Basie). But, when he finally settled back in his hometown, he played mostly traditional jazz. (This is, incidentally, not unique among New Orleans musicians.) Another band that appeared at the Paddock in those days was led by pianist Isaac "Snookum" Russell (1913–1981). That band occasionally included the young trumpeter Jimmy LaRocca, the son of the Original Dixieland Jass Band's Nick LaRocca, and the leader of today's reincarnation of the ODJB.

Wood calls the **Famous Door** a "pitiful shell of what it once was." Yet he also reports that the likes of drummer June Gardner (1930–2010), trumpeter George "Kid Shiek" Colar (1908–1996), and young Swedish clarinetist "Orange" Kellin played there. That rather argues against his initial assessment.

The **Maison Bourbon**, on the so-called "Jazz Corner" of Bourbon and St. Peter streets, featured the bands of veteran trumpeter Thomas Jefferson (1921–1986) in the afternoons and popular Dixieland trumpeter Roy Liberto (1928–2007) in the evenings. Liberto's clarinetist, Tony Mitchell (1916–1999), was another of those fine musicians who, in my opinion, did not get the broader recognition they deserved. Presumably this is due in large part to some New Orleans musicians choosing not to travel widely. Mitchell, however, was not a native New Orleanian, having moved to the city from the Northeast.

The Maison Bourbon, with its well-known sign outside signaling its dedication to "the preservation of jazz," has the longest continuous history as a jazz club on Bourbon Street. It remains among the city's declining number of venues featuring traditional jazz to this day.

Crazy Shirley's was just across the street. The band of bassist and vocalist George French, the son of Papa French and younger brother of drummer Bob French (1937–2012), held forth at that venue. One of his band members was a young Freddie Lonzo, who has deservedly become one of the top trombonists in the city today.

A short distance from the Jazz Corner on St. Peter is **Preservation Hall**, another venue with which Wood was no longer particularly impressed. He admitted that "you can still hear great musicians such as [drummer] Louis Barbarin [1902–1997], [guitarist] Justin Adams [1923–1991], [trumpeter] Kid Thomas [Valentine] [1896–1987], [clarinetist] Raymond Burke [1904–1986], [banjoist] Emanuel Sayles [1907–1986], the immortal [trombonist] Jim Robinson [1892–1976]—and one or two others." But he goes on to say that they rarely play together, instead being "surrounded—again with exceptions—by second-rate musicians who could have never made it up the river to Chicago and whose only musical virtue is simply their age." He adds that "antiquity for antiquity's sake only appeals to antiquarians" Unfortunately, such complaints were not unique to Mr. Wood. But the venue was—and continues to be—a major draw for tourists from all over the world.

Next door to Preservation Hall was a small place known as **Easy Eddie's**. It was managed for a time by Don Marquis and was a popular after-hours place for musicians. Unfortunately, it lasted only a little over a year. Suhor calls it "perhaps the most genial atmosphere in town."[16]

Wood concludes by noting "the place where you can consistently hear the best jazz music in New Orleans today." That would be **Heritage Hall**, which "alternately features the bands of [clarinetist] Louis Cottrell [1911–1978] and [banjoist] Albert 'Papa' French [1910–1977]. The members of both bands, for the most part, have played together for years and, musically, it shows." When either of these bands was out of town, he adds, Danny Barker and his Jazz Hounds filled in. He calls this "the best jazz bargain—all the way around—in New Orleans today." Unfortunately, Heritage Hall, like most of its featured performers and most of the clubs mentioned here, is no longer with us.

Dixieland Hall was dead by the middle of the decade. Preservation Hall outlived them all.

Finally, some of the downtown hotels also offered live jazz. Wood cites, for example, the historic **Monteleone** on Royal Street, "where the current version of the Dukes of Dixieland (no original members included) hold forth when they are in town." That statement perhaps requires a bit of explanation.

The fraternal founders of the Dukes, trumpeter Frankie and trombonist Freddie Assunto, were gone by then, with the death of the former in 1974. (Freddie had passed away in 1966.) And gone with them was the original band, which has resulted in almost endless litigation since that time.[17]

One other hotel deserves mention, the Royal Orleans on St. Louis Street. The **Esplanade Lounge**, rather more than just another piano bar, is located there. At the time of Wood's visit, the remarkable New Orleans pianist Armand Hug (1910–1977) held forth, and the writer rightly notes, "No words are needed to describe his genius, his artistry, nor his contribution to jazz." That was in 1976. Hug died in the following year.

John Royen, a leading stride-pianist in the city today, has a story to tell about that. Raised on the East Coast, Royen moved to New Orleans in 1977 and was enrolled at Loyola University. "The first week I got here," he says, "I had wanted to hear a pianist everybody had told me about, Armand Hug. So, I went down to the Royal Orleans to see him [and learned] Armand had died two days beforehand [March 17]. And there was Don Ewell at the piano! [Royen had known the highly regarded Ewell from his days in Washington, D.C.] Don had just come in to take over Armand's job at the Royal Orleans. He was there five nights a week—and I was there five nights a week! I never went to any classes, I never did any studying. Actually, I did well in all my theory courses, but I dropped a lot of courses because I was too busy listening to Don. That's when we got to be very good friends. I was there every night."[18]

The **Hilton** at the foot of Canal Street added a jazz venue as well. In fact, the Al Belletto quartet opened the lobby bar there in 1977, and the group remained in situ for about another year.[19]

Wood's account clearly focuses on the clubs in the French Quarter that featured traditional or Dixieland jazz. Yet he did not mention other clubs that debuted during the decade of the seventies, such as **Fritzel's European Jazz Pub**, which opened at 631 Bourbon in 1973 and moved four years later to its present location down the block (733 Bourbon). (While the arithmetic doesn't add up, it celebrated what was called its forty-fourth anniversary at that location in October 2013.)

Likewise, the **Gazebo** on Decatur Street, which also featured traditional jazz, opened in 1979. Royen and his good friend, native New Orleans pianist Steve Pistorius, were hired to play solo piano there, on an alternating basis. Royen stayed on for nearly eight years, while Pistorius went on to lead and play with other bands in town.

The **Maple Leaf**, 8316 Oak Street (Uptown), opened in 1974. Unlike today, for the most part, traditional jazz could be heard there. Drummer Andrew Hall's Society Jazz Band, featuring the likes of Chris Clifton on trumpet, played there at least one night a week at the time.

Two more clubs opened in 1977, also not in the French Quarter. The **Dream Palace**, 534 Frenchmen Street in Faubourg Marigny, was purchased in 1976 by Deborah and Alan Langhoff. The Frenchmen Street neighborhood became more popular in the following decade and has remained even more so in this century.

Tipitina's, on the corner of Napoleon and Tchoupitoulas (Uptown), became the home base of the legendary Henry Roeland Byrd (a.k.a. "Professor Longhair"), along with other R&B artists and the occasional jazz group. The club has become something of a legend in its own time because of that.

Unfortunately, it is a truism that jazz clubs come and go. Those that manage to stay in business for years are the exceptions. The **Dew Drop Inn**, a legendary African American music venue at 2840 LaSalle Street (Uptown/Central City), had been a major club for modern jazz and R&B during the '50s and '60s. But it had closed by the early '70s. There were successors, however.

Lu and Charlie's, a restaurant-bar at 1101 N. Rampart Street, was also a popular—perhaps the leading—modern jazz venue at the time (1972–78). Founders Lula Lowe Lewis and Charlie Bering came from St. Louis with the intention of opening a club for modern jazz. Ellis Marsalis worked there quite regularly, along with virtually all of the city's other contemporary jazz players. When Al Belletto's group opened there in 1975, after the Playboy's closing, "there wasn't an empty chair in the house," Rhodes Spedale wrote. "Business was more than brisk; Belletto and his group broke the previous record of business set by James Moody—quite a saxophonist himself. Al Herman, his trombonist, wailed up a storm!" Spedale then continues on the modern jazz scene at the time: "Although Ellis Marsalis, James Black, and others have been playing modern jazz of the Charlie Parker persuasion and beyond for years, I don't believe that the City of New Orleans realized what had happened in jazz since 1945 until that fall, when Belletto and Herman purveyed the sounds of that era at Lu and Charlie's. It was like a catch-up course in modern jazz development."[20]

Ms. Lewis, a charming and enthusiastic lady who now lives in Pensacola, Florida, was back in town in November 2012 for a tribute concert to the club at the Old U.S. Mint. It featured music by a quartet led by guitarist Carl LeBlanc, whose first gig was at Lu and Charlie's. Lu has put together an exhibit which will eventually be housed in a museum in Pensacola, but it is also available to travel to other cities. In the brochure describing the exhibit, Bruce Raeburn of Tulane's Jazz Archive is quoted:

"Lu and Charlie's benefited from an esprit de corps which helped sustain and nurture modern jazz in New Orleans at a crucial stage in its development. It was the life line that made the future possible." Wynton Marsalis adds, "The thing that made me want to be a jazz musician is when I used to hear my father and James Black play at Lu and Charlie's on Rampart Street. . . . what made Lu and Charlie's so fascinating was that it took musicians and put them with listeners, and the two made a special feeling together." And the tributes to the club went on and on.[21]

Another black-owned club, like Lu and Charlie's, was **Mason's VIP Lounge** at 2345 Claiborne Avenue (Uptown/Central City). Opened in the late '60s, it flourished in the '70s and eventually closed in the early '80s. Many of the AFO modernists like saxophonist Red Tyler, bassist Chuck Badie, and pianist Ed Frank, along with former big-band drummer June Gardner, played there on a regular basis. It also featured nationally touring modern-jazz musicians from time to time. There were actually *two* motels by this name owned by the same family operating concurrently. The second, now called the Crescent Palms Motel, is located at 3923 Martin Luther King Boulevard in Central City. It seems, however, that the Claiborne location—the newer of the two—was the site of the performance venue.[22] (The two motels are still in existence today, though operated by two different groups.)

Probably the hottest new band playing contemporary jazz in the city at this time was **Astral Project** (AP), founded by tenor saxophonist Tony Dagradi in 1978. Dagradi, a New Jersey native, attended the prestigious Berklee College of Music in Boston. After leaving New England, his travels took him to New Orleans, where he eventually settled. He has worked with a variety of modern jazz luminaries, including avant-garde pianist and composer Carla Bley, but he is best known for his association with AP, now a co-op band.

Dagradi has been professor of saxophone and jazz studies at Loyola University since 1990. His AP associates are no less distinguished. Ace guitarist Steve Masakowski has been professor of jazz studies and chair of that program at the University of New Orleans since 1992. Versatile bassist James Singleton has long been regarded as one of the first calls in town, and drummer Johnny Vidacovich has a similar reputation. Multitalented pianist David Torkanowsky, whose father was one-time director of the New Orleans Symphony Orchestra and whose mother was a flamenco dancer, was also a founding member of the group, but he left the band in 2003. Another early member of the group was Cuban-influenced percussionist Mark Sanders, a New Yorker who played with AP from 1980 to 1986 (when he returned to New York City). Apart from Dagradi and Singleton (who moved to town from the Midwest, via North Texas State, in 1977), the other members of the group are native New Orleanians. The quartet's music is original, boldly adventurous, and stylistically diverse. They have a national reputation and have toured widely in this country and abroad. Astral Project has made at least seven albums as a group and countless recordings as individuals.[23]

NEW ORLEANS JAZZ AND HERITAGE FESTIVAL (JAZZFEST)

We have seen that the 1969 JazzFest was not a commercial success. But, as Suhor put it, "To the credit of the festival staff, JazzFest has not turned to the blatant commercialism of Newport. In the words of talent director Willis Conover, JazzFest is 'the world's only all-jazz festival.'"[24] But that could not go on forever.

There was another edition of the festival in 1970, and that has been considered the *official* beginning of the "New Orleans Jazz Festival and Louisiana Heritage Fair," as it was then called. The first two years, 1970 and 1971, each took place in late April and lasted only four days. They were money losers, having drawn crowds of only a few hundred.[25] The events took place in Beauregard (Congo) Square in what is now Armstrong Park, the nearby Municipal Auditorium (now officially known as the Morris F. X. Jeff Auditorium), and night-time concerts on the riverboat, the legendary *S.S. President*.

The programs were largely put together by "co-directors" Quint Davis and Allison Miner, students working at Tulane's Jazz Archive and good friends whose backgrounds were principally in pop music, in collaboration with Newport producer George Wein. Rhodes Spedale has also indicated that Al Belletto acted as musical director for a number of the "early versions" of JazzFest.[26] After the first year, Davis and Miner seem to have been essentially in charge of the event until Ms. Miner's death in 1995. Davis, the son of a distinguished New Orleans architect, has been executive director of the festival for years and serves as the CEO of Festival Productions, the organization that produces JazzFest.

The jazz portions of those first two years were in the capable hands of some of the city's top bands (including brass bands). They were complemented by the appearance of notable visiting artists, such as the Duke Ellington Orchestra (1971) and Dizzy Gillespie (1972).

The festival grew to the point that its location was moved to the more spacious Fairgrounds Racetrack in the Bayou St. John neighborhood near City Park in 1972. It has remained there ever since (despite occasional urging by Wein and Davis to move it to the Superdome after it opened in 1975). From 1972 through 1975, the festival took place on a three-day weekend and included night concerts. Attendance seems to have reached 50,000.[27] In 1976, it expanded to two weekends and seven nighttime concerts, and attendance was estimated to have doubled.[28] In 1979, the event's tenth anniversary, a third weekend was added (from Friday, April 20, through Sunday, May 6). In addition to the evening concerts, more stages were added as well. As Kevin McCaffrey notes, "The official 1979 Jazz Fest program boasted that the Fest 'had the potential to become the largest American music Festival in history,' estimating attendance of 300,000." We, of course, do not know the relationship these numbers bore to reality.[29]

An impressive list of "name" jazz talent appeared at JazzFest over the first decade. The names included Ellington, Gillespie, Benny Goodman, Dave Brubeck, Herbie Hancock, Earl Hines, Bobby Hackett, Freddie Hubbard, McCoy Tyner, Ella Fitzgerald, Eubie Blake, Charles Mingus, Sonny Rollins, Lionel Hampton, and Count Basie—not to mention the top local bands (both trad and mod). Beyond that, of course, were the increasing numbers of major pop stars—Stevie Wonder, B. B. King, Gladys Knight, the Staple Singers, Fats Domino, Natalie Cole, and the like—who clearly brought out large crowds. ("More heritage than jazz" is a favorite outcry of the critics of that trend.) Likewise, the organizers have seen the need to rely increasingly on corporate entities for the sponsorship of the event. As of the forty-first installment in 2011, its official name has become "The New Orleans Jazz and Heritage Festival Presented by Shell [Oil]." But to everyone in New Orleans it remains simply "JazzFest."

In addition to bringing name talent to the city as well as bands from all over Europe, Africa, the Far East, and Latin America, JazzFest has performed an important service by providing additional work for most local musicians. A significant number of them, in fact, are lucky enough to have had more than one gig at each festival. Since the first festivals in this country in the 1950s, there has been a proliferation of comparable events both here and abroad (especially throughout Europe)—thus giving further work opportunities to many New Orleans musicians during the slower summer months in the city.[30]

Yet the festival was not without its problems in those early years, most often racially motivated by African Americans who felt that whites were dominating the event. It seems to have reached a peak in 1978, when there were only three African Americans among the Foundation Board of twenty members.[31] Other problems also existed, but Wein and Davis seem to have made sufficient compromises to keep a coalition of black dissenters from causing serious trouble. Since that time, such issues have been minimal, and the African American presence in the administration of the foundation and the festival has increased markedly. Michael Smith concluded, "The manner in which this issue was resolved at the festival was exemplary, and though these sorts of deliberations have not always been easy, it can be said that, in spite of some very understandable frictions the Jazz Fest has served to unite New Orleans more than any other event in the city's history."[32]

Reflecting upon the 1972 event, Don Marquis, the author of the seminal book about Buddy Bolden, had the following observations about the informal jam sessions and get-togethers that took place after the daytime activities of the fest:

> When the New Orleans Jazzfest was first organized no one foresaw the fact that it would someday attract not only people from all over the world to see and listen, but would also attract a goodly number

to play and exchange ideas and music. This, in my opinion, is what makes this particular event so great and so unique. It should be encouraged and developed. The formal concerts are an enjoyable and necessary part of any jazz festival. But when you have as much spontaneous music and so many devoted fans willing to follow the sounds until six or seven in the morning and then come back ready for more by noon you have a rare atmosphere, an atmosphere that should never die for a simple lack of cooperation, coordination and organization. Whatever those of us in New Orleans who hover on the fringes of the official functions can do has been kicked over . . . with the thought in mind that Jazzfest will and must continue to grow bigger and better. There is room for all.[33]

THE NORWEGIAN SEAMEN'S CHURCH: "THE JAZZ CHURCH"

The Norwegian Seamen's Mission is funded and staffed by the Norwegian government to serve Norwegians (mainly sailors originally) in some thirty-one major port cities throughout the world. The church in New Orleans was founded in 1906 and is only one of six such churches remaining in the United States.[34] It is located at 1772 Prytania Street, in the Lower Garden District (Uptown).

The Norwegian Seamen's Church in New Orleans celebrated its 100th anniversary in 2006, the year after the city was devastated by the hurricanes, hosting a visit by Crown Prince Haakon of Norway. Over the years, hundreds of jazz musicians, both local and foreign, have performed in concert or jazz services at the church, as a result of which it has come to be known as *Jazzkirken* (in Norwegian, "the Jazz Church") both here and in Norway (and, indeed, elsewhere as well).

The jazz tradition in the church began during the pastorate of Reverend Paul Daasvand (1970–79), during which time a close relationship developed between the church and Preservation Hall (which was barely a decade old at the time). As it happened, the church's postman in those days was Narvin Kimball (1909–2006). It was not uncommon for him to take a break from his daily rounds and have a coffee and waffle at the church.

When it eventually became known that Kimball was a musician (banjoist and vocalist) and charter member of the Preservation Hall Jazz Band, it is not difficult to understand how the close relationship between Preservation Hall and the church developed and evolved. It began with the church's regular Saturday-night visits—"Jazz and Beef Nights"—to Preservation Hall. Reciprocal visits and performances by the PHJB soon followed, and the rest is history.

Kimball, who was employed by the U.S. Postal Service for thirty-seven years, played at the church many times. He passed away on March 17, 2006, just fifteen days after his ninety-seventh birthday and, unfortunately, just a few months before the church celebrated its centennial. His last performance with the PHJB was in 1999 in a concert aired on public television (PBS). Shortly thereafter (January 2000), he suffered the first of a series of strokes that soon led to the end of his musical career.

The PHJB played its first concert at the church in the spring of 1972, and they have returned many times since. In addition, countless other top New Orleans jazzmen have played at the Seamen's Church during that period. Among those who have made numerous appearances are trumpeter Wallace Davenport (who played the first of seventeen consecutive Good Friday concerts in 1979); famed Norwegian ragtime pianist Morten Gunnar Larsen (who lived and worked in New Orleans for a time as well); gospel/jazz singer Aline White; jazz singer Lillian Boutte (who was also married in the church); trumpeter Gregg Stafford; clarinetist Michael White; trombonist Freddie Lonzo; guitarist/banjoist Don Vappie; Uncle Lionel Batiste (who also served as grand marshal for the Molde Jazz Festival in Norway for many years); pianist Lars Edegran; vocalist Big Al Carson; and clarinetist Tom Fischer. (With all due respect to those not mentioned, these represent but the tip of the iceberg.)

The first Scandinavian band to perform at the church was the fine Swedish big band Kustbandet, which was in town to play at the Jazz and Heritage Festival in the same year (1972). A few years later, the popular and talented Ytre-Suloens Jass-ensemble from Norway was invited to JazzFest. They became the first Norwegian jazz group to appear at the church (1976). Both of those bands have revisited New Orleans many times since then, along with countless other groups from Norway, Sweden, Denmark, Finland, Germany, and other countries in Europe and Asia.[35]

The Seamen's Church continues to host a jazz service on the first Sunday of each month (except in July and August). Beyond that, there is the annual Scandinavian Festival each autumn and a series of concerts during the French Quarter Festival and JazzFest each spring. They have become very popular and well-attended events in the city—and not just for members of the local Scandinavian community.

JAZZ REPERTORY

Despite having their idols and primary influences, good jazz musicians have traditionally aimed to achieve their own sound on their instruments. Yet there have always been times in the past when clarinet players, for example, tried to emulate, if not downright imitate, the sound and style of famous players such as Benny Goodman. In New Orleans—and maybe even more so in Europe during the Trad Revival of the '40s and '50s—New Orleans clarinetist George Lewis (1900–1968) was the object of such imitation. And, of course, this sort of thing applies to virtually all jazz instrumentalists (and vocalists as well): Armstrong's trumpet playing, Kid Ory's trombone style, and so on. This, in a very small way, may have been the origin of what has been called the repertory movement. But, as Hasse has observed in connection with the Smithsonian Jazz Masterworks Orchestra and the music of Duke Ellington, "a big band provides by far the widest range of dynamics, sonorities, and tonal colors" to express a composer's or, I might add, an era's music.[36]

The 1970s seem to have been marked by the formation of a number of bands in the repertory genre. In New Orleans, the **New Orleans Ragtime Orchestra** (NORC), founded by pianist Lars Edegran in 1967, flourished in the '70s and '80s and has continued to perform on special occasions (such as JazzFest) to the present day. The group plays largely music from the ragtime era (ca. 1890 to ca. 1915). It appeared at the Newport Jazz Festival in 1970 (and was recorded there), then toured Europe for six weeks in 1974, and has traveled extensively since that time. Its music is heard on the soundtrack of the 1978 film *Pretty Baby*, starring Brooke Shields.

The composition of the group has varied over time, but earlier editions included Lionel Ferbos, trumpet (who, now in his second century, still performs with NORO); Paul Crawford (1925–1996), trombone; Orange Kellin, clarinet; the eminent jazz historian and avant-garde composer Bill Russell (1905–1992), violin; Walter Payton (1942–2010), bass; John Robichaux (1915–2005), drums; and, of course, Edegran, piano. NORO has made numerous recordings under its own name—something like eight in the period 1967–88—but is heard in other contexts as well. For example, the band can be seen and heard in an excellent 1988 documentary film dedicated to the music of famed New Orleans composer-bandleader Armand Piron (1888–1943). Funded by the Louisiana Endowment for the Humanities, the film is called *The Mystery of the Purple Rose* and is narrated by Vernel Bagneris. Several of the band members also performed in Bagneris's immensely popular stage show, *One Mo' Time*, which debuted in 1978 and continued to be performed—both here and abroad—for years thereafter.

Another band with a similar approach is the **New Leviathan Oriental Foxtrot Orchestra**, which was co-founded in 1972 by artist, banjoist, vocalist, and humorist George Schmidt and jazz historian, saxophonist, and city-planner Jack Stewart. The New Leviathan appears annually at JazzFest, where it has become one of the longest continuously performing musical organizations, and at a variety of other occasions. Now four decades old, it continues to draw an enthusiastic and loyal following to its public appearances. It is a larger ensemble than NORO (fifteen to twenty pieces), which results in its varied personnel, who are largely talented amateurs.

The band takes its name from the *SS Leviathan*, a 1920s transatlantic ocean liner, and its repertoire includes popular (and now often obscure) dance numbers from the late nineteenth century to the early 1930s. The music is presented with authenticity and good humor. The band has recorded at least eleven albums (including two remasterings) between 1972 and 2007. It is also heard on the soundtrack of Woody Allen's 1994 film *Bullets Over Broadway* and has performed in Europe and throughout this country, including an appearance on television's *Saturday Night Live*.

Yet another group about the size of NORO playing traditional New Orleans music is the **Louisiana Repertory Jazz Ensemble** (LRJE), founded by reedman, author, and educator S. Frederick Starr in 1979. This band—and, again, the composition has varied over time—plays what members call "classic New Orleans jazz," including well-known trad standards. But the band's aim is to draw attention to the music of some of the purely New Orleans bands (both black and white) of the early twentieth century that are really only known today by jazz aficionados—groups like the New Orleans Owls, Papa Celestin's Tuxedo Orchestra, the Sam Morgan Band, or the Halfway House Orchestra.

Founding member of the band, drummer John Joyce of the Tulane music faculty, has transcribed much of the music of the Morgan band. "You will hear in the music a uniquely rustic style of New Orleans jazz—an early black jazz that must have evolved before ragtime," he says. "It's virtually church music transferred to instruments, a rare example of early black jazz in the state of evolution. To the pioneering musicians who created it, it was simply dance music."[37] Joyce, who is also editor of Tulane's Hogan Archive's *The Jazz Archivist*, says that the band was founded as the "performing arm" of the Hogan Jazz Archive. They have recorded a half-dozen albums, performed at the Grammy Awards and with a number of symphony orchestras throughout the country as well as at numerous jazz festivals both here and abroad.

Many fine musicians have played with the LRJE over the years. In addition to Starr, recent members include pianist David Boeddinghaus, clarinetist-saxophonist Tom Fischer, banjoist-vocalist John Parker, trombonist Fred Lonzo, cornetists Lew Green and Charlie Fardella, along with Joyce on drums.

Is the era of repertory bands over? That is quite unlikely, in my opinion. As respected jazz educator David Baker has recently said in connection with the Smithsonian Jazz Masterworks Orchestra, "We started out doing music from 1928 to 1938. Then it was 1928 to 1942 and now this season I did music that was written in 1976. Pretty soon repertory music will mean music written over a month ago."[38] Indeed, there will always be good music that has been neglected or overlooked and must be preserved and performed authentically, not least the music of New Orleans.

NEW ORLEANS BRASS BANDS IN THE 1970S

The traditional New Orleans brass bands—groups such as the Onward, the Olympia, the Eureka, the Young Tuxedo, Doc Paulin's Brass Band, and so on—continued to play a significant role in the New Orleans music and the black social-club and funeral-parade scene during this time.

The **Onward Brass Band**, probably the oldest of them, went through several leadership changes during its history. When drummer Paul Barbarin passed away in 1969, clarinetist Louis Cottrell Jr. (1911–1978) took over the leadership. But, with the death of Cottrell in 1978, drummer Placide Adams (1929–2003) assumed the reins, and he remained in that role for the next twenty-five years. (It has recently been revived by drummer Dr. Kurt Nicewander.)

The **Olympia Brass Band** (or "Dejan's Olympia Brass Band") also has its roots in the later nineteenth century. Under the leadership of Harold "Duke" Dejan (assisted increasingly by trumpeter Milton Batiste, who started with the band in the 1960s), it may have been the most popular brass band in the city among both tourists and natives in the '70s, '80s, and '90s. The band has became highly visible through its travels, convention and television appearances.

The **Eureka Brass Band** was founded in 1920 and passed through a series of leaders and sidemen. Trumpeter Percy Humphrey became its leader in 1947 and remained so until the group disbanded in 1975.

The **Young Tuxedo Brass Band**, while historically more recent than the three above, also experienced a leadership change in the '70s, reedman Herman Sherman (1923–1984) taking over when fellow reedman Andrew Morgan (1903–1972) passed away.

Clarinetist and traditional jazz historian Dr. Michael White has written movingly and in some detail about a popular brass band of the era and its legendary leader, "Doc Paulin's Dixieland Jazz Band" (as Paulin himself called it).[39] This is a major historical document and one that is more than an encomium to the venerable trumpeter and bandleader or an autobiographical statement by the author about his introduction to traditional New Orleans jazz. It is an insightful eyewitness look at a critical period—the late 1970s—in New Orleans music history and the related African American experience. White calls it a time of transition "in the history of New Orleans music: the last years that authentic traditional-style jazz served a vital and functional role in the African American community as the dominant music of brass bands in social club parades, church processions and jazz funerals."[40]

While White could write, "Unless one was part of that subculture, it is hard to understand the power and impact that traditional jazz still had in black New Orleans during the mid-1970s,"[41] he also observed that, by the end of the decade, "several changes were in the wind. . . . The middle and late 1970s turned out to be a transition period, after which the look, sound, and feel of brass bands and the parade traditions around them would forever be radically different."[42]

The changes that White was alluding to included the gradual replacement of the older musicians like Doc Paulin by a younger generation with quite different musical roots and experiences. Eventually, the process resulted in what White called "a new revolutionary modern brass band style."[43] He notes, however, that the new style was not born full-blown out of the head of Zeus, having already revealed hints of change in earlier years.

White also happened to be part of another group of young brass-band musicians that first came to the fore at the beginning of the decade. This group was known as the **Fairview Baptist Church Christian Band**, founded by the legendary Danny Barker, who had a close association with the Onward Brass Band (among many other musical groups), and the Reverend Andrew Darby of Fairview Baptist Church.[44] Their aim in this endeavor was to make the kids (most of whom were in their early teens at the outset) aware of their cultural and musical heritage.

There is some confusion about the date of the beginning of the Fairview Band. I interviewed Reverend Darby in 2004, and his recollections of some of the relevant circumstances are worthy of note. When asked about the original date, he responded:

> I could say anytime from '69 to '70 because that was when we first started parading. We paraded around the neighborhood. The first year Danny Barker brought a lot of renowned musicians that came around and did our first Easter parade. We used to form in the St. Bernard Project and have our outside services, and he would bring in a lot of [good musicians]. I think a guy named Cottrell, Barbarin, a lot of old guys.
>
> But how the band really got started, Danny just came and joined the church. I didn't really invite him. I just met him at the church. And he said, while he was sitting in the church, he looked up on the choir stand and the members of the choir transformed into his family that had passed on, like angels on the choir stand. He said they were beckoning him, you know. He had a vision while he was sitting in church. And he came up and joined, and I baptized him and he became a part of our fellowship. Both he and his wife were Catholic, and they joined. Well, Lu Blue [*sic*] sang in the choir for a long time, and Danny would always work with the band.[45]

In light of these comments, especially when combined with the recollections of many of the principal musicians themselves, it seems fair to conclude that the band started out at least in 1970, if not a bit earlier.[46] Among the original members were trumpeter Leroy Jones (age thirteen) and trombonist (playing drums) Lucien Barbarin, also thirteen.[47] They were soon joined by trumpeter Gregg Stafford, clarinetist Joe Torregano, then trumpeter (now drummer) Herlin Riley, tubaist Anthony "Tuba Fats" Lacen (1951–2004), the total number eventually reaching nearly thirty, causing the band to split up into sub-groups.[48] Many of these young men have obviously become leading professional musicians in the city (and beyond) today. The Fairview band became extremely popular in the early 1970s, playing at JazzFest already in 1971 and at the Armstrong memorial later in the same year. They made many local appearances as well as playing gigs out of town.

In 1974, **Leroy Jones** decided to go out on his own—at the age of sixteen. "Then I met musicians," he says, "like Kirk Joseph, Charles Joseph, Gregory Davis, and, I almost forgot, saxophonist Kevin Harris who still plays with the Dirty Dozen [Brass Band]. We started doing different things. Tuba Fats was still there. We started venturing away from the traditional repertoire and started making up songs and riffs that hadn't been played yet—Tuba Fats was very instrumental in that—certain riffs on the sousaphone or tuba that they still use in the so-called contemporary brass bands today. We were doing this then."[49]

"And at that time," he goes on, "we switched over to more of a comfortable attire, and we had T-shirts made with 'Leroy Jones Hurricane Brass Band, New Orleans, Louisiana,' with all the information like they would put on the bass drum. Between 1974 and 1976 we were the hottest thing on the street."[50] They also traveled extensively, performing at the Smithsonian Institution and the Kennedy Center in Washington, D.C., and they appeared in a film called *The Minstrel Man*. The band recorded an LP in 1975, *Leroy Jones and His Hurricane Marching Brass Band of New Orleans*. This band clearly made a major contribution to the brass-band "revolution" that Michael White wrote about.

That revolution was carried a step further with the formation of the **Dirty Dozen Brass Band** in 1977, some members of which had been in the Hurricane.[51] One of them was trumpeter Greg Davis, who had met Leroy Jones in high school and became the leader of the new band. Other members of the early core band were Efrem Towns, trumpet; baritone saxophonist Roger Lewis; tenor saxophonist Kevin Harris; Charles (trombone) and Kirk (tuba) Joseph; Jenell Marshall, snare drum; and Benny Jones (now the leader of the Treme Brass Band), bass drum. They were an eight-piece band, smaller than the standard ten-piece traditional brass bands, and their music—a unique mixture of the old and the new—was also noticeably different from the traditional bands. "By spicing up the repertoire with bebop and R&B and by devising novel arrangements, they invented a new form: a contemporary jazz octet that played funky rhythms in a turn-of-the-century instrumental configuration."[52]

According to Davis, the Dirty Dozen began essentially as a rehearsal band because there wasn't much work around town. "All of Bourbon Street had turned disco," he says. "There was no live music anywhere."[53]

They eventually got some gigs, most notably at the Glass House, a tiny club on South Saratoga Street (Uptown), but it wasn't really until the following decade that the band and their reputation began to take off.

JAZZ EDUCATION IN THE 1970S

Brass bands such as the Fairview or Doc Paulin's were great training grounds for aspiring young jazz musicians, as was growing up in musical families like the Barbarins, Bruniouses, Lasties, Paulins, or a host of others. This, plus just standing outside the entrances to jazz clubs or working with veteran musicians on "The Street" (which Pete Fountain called his "university" education), was the traditional way in which young musicians in New Orleans got their jazz educations. (A number of the early Creole musicians, of course, had more formal musical training.) The situation, however, began to change noticeably by the 1970s.

Discussing the teaching methods of the great jazz educator David Baker, J. B. Dyas wrote, "On the first day [of class], David begins by dispelling typical jazz myths, the foremost being that jazz cannot be taught, a misconception often used by jazz professionals who do not know how to teach, and an excuse by music teachers who do not teach their students how to improvise. As David puts it, the adage 'You either got it or you ain't' no longer flies."[54]

While not every jazz musician may totally agree with that, such has been pretty much the case throughout the country since North Texas State (now the University of North Texas) became the first American university to offer a degree in jazz studies in 1947. That gradually caught on at other colleges and universities and soon became a trend across the country. It led to the creation of professional organizations for the teachers of jazz such as the National Association of Jazz Educators (1968), which became the International Association for Jazz Education (1989). The latter went bankrupt and folded in 2009, but it was revived on a slightly less ambitious scale by the Jazz Education Network (JEN) in 2010. (The second annual meeting of the latter convened in New Orleans in January 2011.)

A related group, devoted to the teaching and preservation of traditional jazz—the Traditional Jazz Education Network (TJEN)—had begun some years earlier. It was founded and is run by Dave Robinson, who regularly produced a column on the operation's activities in *The Mississippi Rag*.

After the Second World War, many talented veterans came back home and enrolled in the Music School at Loyola University. Some were very good musicians already but there was no formal jazz program to which they could sign on. In fact, there seems to have been open resistance to jazz among some critical members of the music faculty at Loyola. (This was not an unusual circumstance in music schools in the early years of jazz education.) Nevertheless, the students managed to form some very good jazz ensembles and, by the mid-1960s, the school officially recognized the "Stage Band" by appointing a director with faculty status and giving course credit to members of the group. Mr. Joseph Hebert, who is now director of bands at Loyola, was the director of that band. In his second year in that position he changed the name from "Stage" to "Jazz Band." He says that he was tired of pretending it to be otherwise. Yet there was still no jazz-studies program at the university.[55] That did not come about until 1975. In 1978, the current coordinator of jazz studies, trombonist/pianist/composer John Mahoney, was hired fresh out of Eastman School of Music, and he was named to head up the program in the following year. Jazz studies at Loyola has evolved and grown considerably since those early days.[56]

In the meantime, the first formal jazz program on the secondary public-school level in the city was founded (with the appointment of faculty) in 1973 and officially opened to students in January 1974.[57] This was but a component (though a very important one) of a larger high-school program in the arts broadly—dance, music (both classical and jazz, instrumental and vocal), theater, visual arts, and creative writing—called the New Orleans Center for the Creative Arts. Now widely known simply by its acronym "NOCCA," it was the product of years of difficult and dedicated work by a host of local musicians and educators. Most notable among them, as Al Kennedy has shown, was Ms. Shirley Trusty (Corey) of the Orleans Parish School System. Kennedy describes her as the indefatigable prime mover and perhaps most deserving of the credit for the eventual establishment of the school. But many others—not least clarinetist Alvin Batiste of Southern University in Baton Rouge—made very important contributions along the way.

NOCCA's first home was on the campus of the University of New Orleans, then known as Louisiana State University in New Orleans (LSUNO). (The music and theater arts programs seem to have been located at LSUNO while the visual arts program was at the New Orleans Museum of Art.) Unfortunately, that situation was to last but one year. Therefore NOCCA's first permanent home was established the following year in the recently closed LaSalle Elementary School building at 6048 Perrier Street near Audubon Park, Uptown. (The structure was, at the time of this writing, being converted into condominiums.) Though in need of repair, the building served as the school's home until it moved to its present riverside campus at 2800 Chartres Street in the Bywater neighborhood in 2000.

Dr. Bert Braud, a respected professional musician and composer, was head of the Music Department from the very outset. But the jazz program became the domain of the well-known jazz pianist Ellis Marsalis Jr. in 1975. Prior to that appointment, he had been teaching courses in African American music at Xavier University. With Marsalis's arrival, the NOCCA jazz program immediately gained a solid reputation and turned out its first graduates in that year. Many of the program's alumni were to become significant figures in the jazz realm. The list includes the director's own sons, Branford (1978) and Wynton (1979), who were among the earliest graduates, along with Donald Harrison Jr. (1978). Since those early days, a virtually endless number of outstanding players have distinguished themselves (and their training ground) as NOCCA alumni.

DONALD M. MARQUIS

There were many key figures in the New Orleans jazz community of scholars and researchers after World War II. Their number would include, at the very least, Dick Allen (1927–2007) and Bill Russell (1905–1992) of the Tulane University Jazz Archive and Dr. Edmond "Doc" Souchon (1897–1968) of the New Orleans Jazz Club. While both Allen and Russell continued to play important roles into the decade under consideration here, in my opinion, Don Marquis deserves special recognition as one of the most significant during the 1970s.

Born in Goshen, Indiana, in 1933, Marquis moved to New Orleans in 1962 after serving in the U.S. Navy, graduating from Goshen College, and spending a brief time working in Cleveland, Ohio. He had been a dedicated jazz fan since his teenage years and early developed a burning passion for New Orleans jazz and its musicians. He had, in fact, become a member of the New Orleans Jazz Club (NOJC) long before moving to the city.[58]

Upon arriving in New Orleans he threw himself full bore into the local music scene and quickly became friends with many of the musicians. He worked briefly for the *Times-Picayune,* then for the New Orleans Public Library. The latter became an unexpectedly important and unique resource for his research interests. As a longtime member of the NOJC, he contributed articles to their periodical, *The Second Line,* and was elected to the board of the organization.

The year 1978 seems to have been something of a turning point in his life. As he later put it, "At age 45, life began for me." Number one, his important book, *In Search of Buddy Bolden: First Man of Jazz,* was published by Louisiana State University Press in that year. It received highly favorable reviews in the jazz community, not to mention receiving the Louisiana Literary Award for the same year. (A revised and augmented edition appeared in 2005.) The original was followed in the same year by *Finding Buddy Bolden: The Journal of a Search for the First Man of Jazz* (Pinchpenny Press, Goshen College, 1978).

Secondly, his regular contributions to *The Second Line* led then-editor Myra Menville to ask him to succeed her in that capacity. She soon passed away, and Don's first issue as the magazine's new editor appeared in the spring of 1979. The magazine was named "Best Jazz Publication" by the American Federation of Jazz Societies in 1987. Don retired as editor in 1991 after more than a decade in the financially demanding job. (The reader will readily see how critical that resource has been in the preparation of this book by simply perusing the bibliography.)

Thirdly, the Louisiana State Museum had just inherited the NOJC "jazz museum" materials, and the collection needed a qualified person to oversee its organization, continuation, and expansion. Museum Director Robert McDonald almost immediately named Don to the position of jazz curator for the new museum.

So, it is not surprising that Marquis saw 1978 as the beginning of a new life for himself. "I [became] an author, an editor and now, a curator," he later wrote.[59] He called it "a tremendous challenge," but it also "opened up a lot of world-wide adventures for me." Indeed, it led to travels to lecture and/or attend special events in Japan, Australia, England, France, Germany, The Netherlands, Denmark, Sweden, and Brazil—and some of those countries more than once. (This shows, at least in part, how much New Orleans and its music mean to audiences around the world.) There are few in the jazz world who do not know his name and his work.

Don retired from his curatorial position at the museum in 1996, but he has remained very much involved in the local jazz scene in a variety of capacities right up to the present day. For example, he continues to give Bolden talks at a variety of events at home and throughout the country and remains in charge of the brass-band stage at the French Quarter Festival.

To return, finally, to the 1970s, Marquis had some interesting observations to make in a late '70s interview with jazz writer Gilbert Erskine.[60] In response to a question regarding the "uniqueness" of New Orleans in terms of its race relations after the Civil War and if, as some had maintained, it was due to the tolerance of the prevailing Catholic religion, Marquis (a Catholic) said:

> Some scholars have noted that the lack of neighborhood segregation was strictly economical, but I disagree with that. My research, of course, was done in the area directly pertaining to Buddy Bolden and his family and I did not find economical status to be the predominant reason that Blacks and Whites lived next door to each other and that they apparently got along relatively well. Having lived in New Orleans for over seventeen years, I, personally, have found that there is

> a definite "live-and-let-live" philosophy existing. Where it came from, I do not know, but it does exist. One might not necessarily like, or even know, who lives next door, but if they don't "bug" you, you don't "bug" them.
>
> I do not believe that this phenomena [*sic*] came about entirely because of Catholicism. New Orleans, because of its climate, its low level and swampiness, has always been a rather difficult place to live. The city also has a uniqueness that can only be experienced, not described. I sort of think that these mystical, indefinable qualities have a lot to do with inter-personal and inter-racial relationships.

Such was the decade of the 1970s in New Orleans. There were many new and important developments in the local jazz community. It deserved to be called a time of hope, as Mayor Moon Landrieu so aptly put it early on.

Albert "Papa" French and the Original Tuxedo Jazz Band, 1971. *Left to right,* Bob French, Jeannette Kimball, Joseph "Cornbread" Thomas, French (*sitting*), Clive Wilson, Homer Eugene, and Frank Fields. The name of the band persists to the present day, thus making it the longest continuously performing jazz band in New Orleans. *Photograph courtesy of Gerald French.*

The original (that is, before the post-Katrina repair) statue of Louis Armstrong in Armstrong Park.

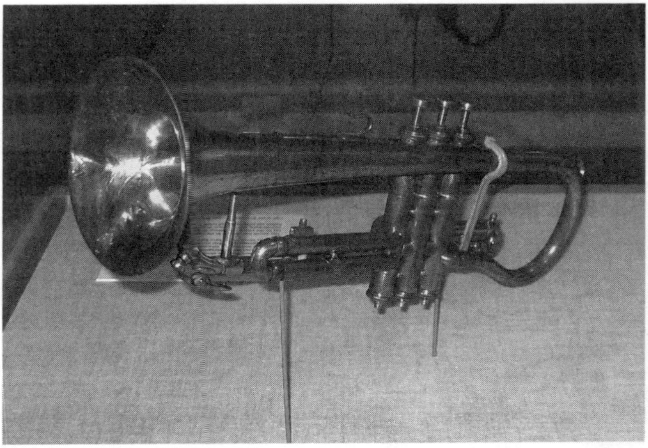

Louis Armstrong's cornet in the Louisiana State Museum (Old U.S. Mint), New Orleans.

Tad Jones is credited with the discovery of the correct date of Louis Armstrong's birthday. He is seen here discussing his discovery at the Jazz Park's Visitor Center.

The intersection of Bourbon and St. Peter streets in the French Quarter was once known as “the jazz corner.” At the right is the venerable Maison Bourbon. Across Bourbon Street was Crazy Shirley’s (now the Krazy Korner). Eddie Bayard’s Jazz Alley was across St. Peter Street from Maison Bourbon.

Lu and Charlie’s was probably the leading modern jazz club in the city in the 1970s. It was located in this building at 1101 North Rampart Street, now the New Orleans Courtyard Hotel.

Ellis Marsalis at Tyler's Beer Garden. Marsalis became the director of the jazz program at the New Orleans Center for the Creative Arts in 1975. Later he headed the jazz studies program at the University of New Orleans. *Photograph courtesy of Fred Laredo.*

Quint Davis, seen in this 1999 photo, has had a major hand in the direction of the New Orleans Jazz and Heritage Festival since the 1970s.

Trombonist John Mahoney, seen here performing with his big band at JazzFest, has headed the Loyola University jazz studies program since the late 1970s.

Astral Project, founded in 1978, continues to be a leading modern jazz unit. Here the group is seen in performance at JazzFest 1999. Tony Dagradi is the saxophonist, with David Torkanowsky on piano, James Singleton on bass, and Steve Masakowski on guitar. Drummer Johnny Vidacovich is not visible here.

The Louisiana Repertory Jazz Ensemble was founded by Fred Starr in the late 1970s. Seen in this JazzFest performance are Fred Lonzo, trombone; Duke Heitger, trumpet; Lew Green, trumpet; Starr, clarinet; Jacques Gauthé, saxophone; and the late John Chaffe, banjo.

The New Leviathan Oriental Foxtrot Orchestra was founded in 1972. Its co-founder George Schmidt is seen here dancing to the music of the orchestra with Helen Arlt in an appearance at Coliseum Square in 1996.

The Norwegian Seamen's Church on Prytania Street in the Lower Garden District. Oftentimes referred to as the "Jazz Church," it has been an integral part of the New Orleans scene for more than a hundred years.

Narvin Kimball, *standing in foreground,* and the Preservation Hall Jazz Band at JazzFest 1997. Kimball was a seminal figure in introducing jazz to the Norwegian Seamen's Church. The PHJB has performed at the church many times over the years. Seen with Kimball are, *from the left,* Frank Demond, trombone; Wendell Brunious, trumpet; David Grillier, clarinet; Ben Jaffe, bass; and Rickie Monie, piano.

Trumpeter Wallace Davenport, at seventy, leads his sixteenth annual Good Friday celebration at the Norwegian Seamen's Church. He began the tradition in 1979.

The first permanent home of the New Orleans Center for the Creative Arts was in this building at 6048 Perrier Street, the former LaSalle School, now in the process of being turned into condominiums.

Don Marquis, with a familiar companion, at the French Quarter Festival 1994.

The Dirty Dozen Brass Band is as popular today as it was more than thirty years ago, and its original core musicians remain largely intact.

3

New Orleans Exposed to the World

THE 1980S

The decade of the 1980s was a time of transition and change in the city. In several notable respects, it was the reverse of the 1970s in New Orleans. In the first place, low energy prices brought on by the "oil bust" meant that the state's economy, so heavily dependent upon the oil industry, was severely crippled. Oil prices dropped to as low as ten dollars a barrel, thus contributing to an unemployment rate of well over 10 percent, the highest in the nation. Commercial activities in the city were severely curtailed, and downtown businesses—especially in the once-flourishing shopping district on Canal Street—were closing rapidly. Yet there was some reason for optimism on the horizon by the end of the decade since deepwater-drilling technology was being developed to give hope to the slumping land-based oil industry.[1]

One big hope for stimulating the local economy was the great **Louisiana World Exposition of 1984**. It was located on a site of more than eighty acres in the run-down and drug-infested area of warehouses (Warehouse District, Arts District today) along the Mississippi River downtown. While the event succeeded in cleaning up an urban slum and creating an upscale neighborhood of apartment complexes and art galleries, its major lasting achievement was perhaps the ever-enlarging Ernest N. Morial Convention Center, which began as part of the "World's Fair" (as the exposition came to be called locally). The convention center has become one of the largest in the nation and is clearly an important resource for a city increasingly dependent upon tourism in all its manifestations. The fair lasted from May 12 to November 11, 1984, and officials expected that it would draw eleven million people to the city in those six months. As it happened, however, just seven million turned out. The multi-million-dollar project ultimately lost over $100 million. Obviously, it represented an additional setback for the local economy.

The theme of the fair was "The World of Rivers—Fresh Water as a Source of Life." As Joan Garvey and Mary Lou Widmer point out, "Although the fair lost a great deal of money, it left a valuable legacy to the people of New Orleans in the development of the riverfront, the construction of hotels and parks, and the improvement of roads." Among the innovations along the riverfront at the end of the decade were the Riverwalk Shopping Mall, Woldenberg Riverfront Park (1989), and the Aquarium of the Americas (1990), all of which clearly were important touristic draws. Woldenberg Park has become an important component of the French Quarter Festival as well as serving as a venue for other musical events.[2] The two mayors during this decade were Ernest N. Morial (1978–86) and Sidney J. Barthelemy (1986–94).

Floyd Levin could write that local restaurants and hotels "were still reeling from the financially disastrous 1984 World's Fair" in the summer of 1985.[3] And Don Marquis, bemoaning the situation at the Louisiana State Museum in his *Second Line* editorial, observed, "1986 was a disastrous year for the State of Louisiana and the City of New Orleans financially. The City [services] is down to four days a week. The State cut backs have affected the Jazz Collection at the Mint even more seriously. The Exhibit is open to the public only on Thursday, Friday and Saturday. In my full time job as Curator of that Collection, it is depressing to see the number of people from all over the world who are turned away on the off days."[4]

But things arguably began to get better as the decade progressed. The World's Fair seems to have been something of an artistic success from the musical standpoint. While I was not a witness to it (having been in town to attend a NASA conference just a year earlier and thereby experience my first Mardi Gras), many eyewitness accounts testify to the abundance of music available to fair-goers.[5] Under the supervision of Charlie Bering (of Lu and Charlie's and Charlie B's fame), who was the manager of music programming for the fair, an impressive lineup of domestic and foreign jazz ensembles appeared at a variety of venues. Marquis mentions "Pete Fountain's Reunion Hall," where bands led by George French,

Banu Gibson, Chuck Credo, Herb Tassin, and, of course, Fountain conducting his own band appeared every day. "Pete, himself, appears very proud of the place, and it is a rare day when he does not show up in person and/or sit in for a few numbers. On Memorial Day week-end," Marquis continues, "at the Amphitheatre [a popular five-million-dollar open-air venue that was torn down after the fair concluded], the following big names appeared: Cab Calloway conducting Count Basie's Orchestra, Dizzy Gillespie, Wynton Marsalis with Trummy Young and the Louis Armstrong Revival Band, Joe Williams, Chris Barber, Duke Ellington Orchestra, Freddie Hubbard, Art Blakey, Woody Herman, Al Hirt, Sarah Vaughan, Preservation Hall Band, Buddy Rich, Billy Taylor, Pete Fountain, and Mel Torme." And that was on just one weekend out of the six-month event!

Helen Arlt mentions other venues—the Jazz & Gospel Tent, the Frey Gazebo, the Italian Village, the German beer garden, the Louisiana Folklife Stage, the "ever-changing, always pleasing Mississippi Pavilion's offerings"—and the musicians featured at those sites. She also goes on to recount the many activities that were going on in the clubs around town during the time of the fair. In short, Arlt concludes, "The Louisiana World Exposition, the Fair in New Orleans, has just closed. It was a glorious six months and tops might have been the abundance of [musical] talent available throughout the day and evening."[6] Unfortunately, the financial return did not measure up to the artistic quality of the event.

AN OVERVIEW OF THE 1980S CLUB SCENE

It is not entirely clear at this point how the local jazz scene was affected by the economic downturn of the '80s. There were complaints that the locals were not supporting the bands (for economic reasons?),[7] but it seems that tourism was at a reasonably high level. Many of the top venues remained in business, but a few dropped by the wayside.[8] What is most striking to me is the increased number of hotels that offered jazz (including jazz brunches), which suggests to me that tourism was not significantly affected by the local economic downturn. Indeed, jazz brunches seem to be one of the musical characteristics of this decade.[9] But these brunches were not the only way in which local hotels provided musicians with work opportunities.

In terms of hotel jazz, I think immediately of the **Hilton** at the foot of Canal Street, where Pete Fountain's splendid new club was located. The hotel later added a trio headed by popular vocalist Sandy Cash (Hancock) six nights a week for a while, then yet another band headed by guitarist/banjoist Vic Tooker five nights a week before hiring talented vocalist Banu Gibson's fine group in the spring of 1989. Then there was the venerable **Monteleone** on Royal Street, where the new Dukes of Dixieland played six nights a week until they were terminated in the summer of 1985, having been replaced by Placide Adams's Heritage Hall Jazz Band on Sunday nights (who were in turn replaced by Mike Carrubba's band on Sundays and Mondays). The **Marriott** on Canal Street featured the wonderful Alvin Alcorn Trio, with Clarence Ford and Jerry Adams, in the lobby bar five nights a week for many years until Alcorn's health forced him out, leaving the duo of Ford and Adams to continue. The **Hyatt Regency** also had the Heritage Hall Jazz Band led by trumpeter Teddy Riley five nights a week, but it was later replaced by clarinetist Chuck Credo's Basin Street Six for a short time on Saturday nights only. **The Columns** on St. Charles Avenue (Uptown) had Andrew Hall's Society Jazz Band one night a week. In 1984, the **International Hotel** on Canal Street introduced a quartet that included Leroy Jones, Ed Frank, Shannon Powell, and F. A. Casano for nightly performances for a brief time. The Louisiana Repertory Jazz Ensemble played Tuesday nights at the **Lafayette Hotel** on St. Charles (Downtown). The **Meridien** on Canal Street embarked on an ambitious and impressive program in mid-decade, rotating six top-notch bands nightly. It became a major venue for traditional jazz for a good period of time. Herb Tassin's Big Band started a six-night per week gig at the **Fairmont** (formerly the Roosevelt, and now the Roosevelt again) in 1986, but the big band was replaced by a trio led by Teddy Riley one night a week in 1989. Trumpeter Gregg Stafford began a run of Sunday brunches at the **Intercontinental** on Poydras Street in 1984 that has continued to the present day. Versatile pianist Willie Metcalf appeared daily at the **Royal Orleans**, Royal and St. Louis. And so it went.

Clearly, there was a good deal of "flexibility" with these programs. But, in my opinion, the Hilton and the Meridien were definitely the standouts where much of the action was consistently taking place at the time. I can remember, for example, a short time in early 1989 when the Hilton featured *four* music venues in the same building at the same time: Pete Fountain's club, of course; Banu Gibson and her Hot Jazz in the French Garden bar; young and upcoming clarinetist Tim Laughlin at Kabby's for Sunday brunch; and the Alan White Trio featuring another fine young clarinetist by the name of Jim Snyder in Winston's dining room. For a clarinet freak like myself, I could hear Fountain, Tom Fischer (with Gibson), Laughlin, and Snyder in one convenient locale. What a treat! And, of course, there were the many hotel piano bars as well.[10]

Then there were the jazz clubs themselves. Many of the old standbys remained in place, but some took on a new look. The **Blue Angel** featured Connie Jones's Crescent City Jazz Band in the late afternoons, with George Finola's Chosen Few in the evenings, until there was a fire that closed the club temporarily in 1984. It reopened briefly, then quit offering traditional jazz in the following year and closed for good in 1986—a big loss, in my opinion. The legendary **Paddock Lounge** also closed and was replaced by **Mahogany Hall**, with daily trad jazz—the fine young cornetist Scott Black made a very good impression on me—and the Dukes of Dixieland appeared occasionally on Sunday nights. The **Famous Door** continued in business, but it seems to have discontinued offering live trad before the end of the decade. The **Maison Bourbon**, with as many as three different bands (for example, bands led by drummer Bob French or trumpeters Wallace Davenport, Roy Liberto, or Murphy Camp) rotating during the day and night, maintained its busy schedule throughout the decade. Needless to say, **Preservation Hall** (featuring at least four different bands during the course of the weeknights) remained a headquarters for the "authentic" jazz-seeking tourists.[11] **Crazy Shirley's**, 640 Bourbon, featured trumpeters Wallace Davenport and Tommy Yetta.

There were some new clubs as well. Cornetist Eddie Bayard, back in town after many years playing the Mississippi riverboats, opened a club in 1980 on the "Jazz Corner" (Bourbon and St. Peter) called **Bayard's Jazz Alley** (701 Bourbon Street). He learned some lessons from that experiment. "I started out by having the house band," he says, "but I soon realized you cannot run a club from the bandstand. It's a full-time job. When you own a club, you're married to it. I put a lot of 18-hour days in the place. You can't concentrate on the music when you've got your mind on everything else. So, I just decided not to do it. I'd rather walk around the club and be the host or manager."[12]

The decision proved to be a big break for what turned out to be one of the hottest new bands in town, Banu Gibson and her New Orleans Hot Jazz. "It was a Wednesday night [in 1981]," Bayard recalls. "What happened was, I was playing there and I had a gig with the Repertory band [the Louisiana Repertory Jazz Ensemble], so I asked Banu if she could put together a band to sub on the Wednesday night. She said she thought she could, so she got Charlie Fardella [cornet], Dickie Taylor [drums], and I think it was Steve Pistorius [piano] and a bunch of other people. I don't think she'd fronted a group before. After my gig was over, I went back to the club and listened to her. It sounded good. So, I said to her, 'It sounds so good, why don't you just keep it.' So, that's how the New Orleans Hot Jazz was born."

Bayard's club didn't last long, but he gave it one more shot in 1984—in the same building. Yet that, too, failed to last. In a little more than a year, "Eddie Bayard's Jazz Alley, the Jazz Corner of the World," had been transformed into a club featuring rock-and-roll music—thanks largely to his new partner who owned 100 percent of the lease. Bayard's conclusion about owning a jazz club? "I wouldn't want to run one again," he asserts firmly.

By the last years of the decade, **Fritzel's European Jazz Pub**, 733 Bourbon Street, was hosting clarinetist Chris Burke's trio (with John Royen on piano and Barry Martyn on drums) every Friday and Saturday night.

Spedale mentions **Germaine Welles' Lounge**, 833 Bienville Street, as having "all the makings of a jazz club," including "a seedy atmosphere" and a "battle-worn piano." But some fine modern pianists like James Drew, Michael Pellera, and David Torkanowsky were known to tickle those ivories.

Moving down from the heart of Bourbon Street to Decatur Street, a popular open-air venue was the **Gazebo** and its next-door neighbor, the **Mediterranean Café** (the former Morning Call and present Market Café). Young clarinetist Michael White, along with trumpeter Gregg Stafford and veteran pianist Sadie Goodson Colar, could often be heard at the latter. But both locales had good music and were popular sites for jazz fans during the daytime hours on weekends. **Bonaparte's Retreat**, just across Decatur Street, was another favorite hangout for locals and foreign bands and visitors—something of a precursor to Fritzel's in the following decade—on the weekends.

Storyville Jazz Hall (now Margaritaville), 1104 Decatur Street, opened in 1984. A large space, it featured traditional jazz nightly from 8 p.m. to midnight, with a rotation of four fine bands led by Chris Burke, Placide Adams, Teddy Riley, and Clive Wilson.

Still farther down Decatur—1204, to be exact—what was to become a *major* new home for traditional jazz opened in January 1989. The **Palm Court Jazz Café** was the brainchild of George and Nina Rimington Buck.

Growing up in the Southeast, the now legendary George H. Buck Jr. was a jazz maven from an early age. Indeed, he founded the Jazzology record label at the relatively tender age of twenty-one. Since that time, he has acquired another half-dozen or more smaller, independent jazz record labels. He has also been deeply involved in the owning and acquisition of radio stations in the southeastern United States. To make a long and very impressive story somewhat shorter, George tired of running his Jazzology business out of Columbia, South Carolina, and Atlanta. He and Nina bought a home in the French Quarter in 1986, and George began to move his entire operation to the Crescent City. New Orleans became their home. Nina would oversee the management of the restaurant, and George, with assistants, ran his business interests and the George H. Buck Jr. Jazz Foundation (begun in 1984) from rooms above the restaurant/club.

Almost from the very beginning (pianist Butch Thompson played for the private opening on January 11, 1989), the Palm Court offered live jazz—eventually five nights a week, including the weekends, with a band led by veteran trombonist Louis Nelson (1902–1990). In addition to its attractive menu of local cuisine, the club rapidly became the headquarters of all—both local and visitors—who had more than a passing interest in New Orleans jazz. The Palm Court, by now, has arguably become the leading club featuring traditional jazz in the city.[13] The arrival of the Buck empire has to be one of the most significant happenings on the city's music scene in the 1980s. The contributions of both George and Nina to the New Orleans jazz community over the years since that time have been enormous and cannot be overstated.

Moving still farther along down Decatur and crossing Esplanade, one leaves the French Quarter and enters Faubourg Marigny. The first main street to be encountered is Frenchmen Street, which, in the decade of the 1980s, had already come to presage what was to become essentially the musical successor to Bourbon Street.

The **Dream Palace** debuted in 1977 but then fell into virtual musical disuse until it reopened in 1988. The New Leviathan Oriental Foxtrot Orchestra was playing there one night a week during at least part of the '80s as part of an eclectic musical menu. Only a few doors away, the **Faubourg** opened shortly thereafter (1980) and featured modern jazz. Among the groups that played there were guitarist Steve Masakowski, Astral Project, saxophonist Earl Turbinton, and a Latin group called Caliente including the fine Cuban percussionist Hector Gallardo. Faubourg's life span was short, however, closing in the fall of 1982.

Faubourg's successor on that site, **Snug Harbor**, 626 Frenchmen Street, which opened in late 1982, ultimately came to be synonymous with modern jazz in the city. Initially, however, its offerings were limited and more varied and even featured the likes of Danny Barker and his Jazz Hounds on Wednesday nights.[14] Yet, while the likes of pianist Ellis Marsalis and modern saxophonists Red Tyler and Earl Turbinton soon became regulars, management chose to offer a more diverse musical menu. It's somewhat disheartening to hear co-owner Glen Menish admit: "There are not enough people looking for modern jazz to support *one* modern jazz club. . . . we just can't have it every night."[15]

Menish left Snug in late 1991, and George Brumat replaced him as business manager. Jason Patterson also returned as musical director (after a hiatus since 1985). He calls the following period, until the death of Brumat in 2007, the "Golden Age" of Snug Harbor.

It is clear that the musical center of gravity had already begun to shift away—mainly "lakeward"—from Canal and Bourbon streets. Moving still farther downstream from the Marigny, one reaches the Bywater neighborhood and the Upper Ninth Ward. There, in 1981, was founded **Vaughan's**, a musical venue that has remained on site ever since and has become something of a legend. It ultimately came to be known as the home of trumpeter Kermit Ruffins and his band (the Barbecue Swingers) who, at the time of this writing, had been playing there for eighteen consecutive years.

For a brief period in the late '80s, even the Warehouse District got into the act. **O'Connell & Flynn**, a restaurant with a "club room," hired the fine modern jazz pianist James Drew, who had only recently returned to town, and top-flight bassist Bill Huntington (Dewey Sampson sat in for the latter on occasion) for duo performances Friday and Saturday nights. There were hopes, it seems, that eventually the group would be enlarged. Unfortunately, the experiment did not last long enough to see that happen, and the club folded.

A well-known and very popular Uptown club was **Tyler's Beer Garden**, 5220 Magazine Street. Called "something of a cultural landmark," it was another of the few places to hear modern jazz in the city. Tyler's was acquired and managed by Fred Laredo in the late '70s and became very popular in the '80s, especially with jazz fans and Uptown college students from Loyola and Tulane. Unfortunately, it closed in 1991 and was subsequently badly damaged by fire. It ceased to be a nightclub thereafter and was later restored to serve another commercial purpose.[16] Jason Patterson observes, "Once **Lu and Charlie's** closed, Snug became the downtown modern jazz club and Tyler's its uptown equivalent."

Ellis Marsalis was one of the musicians who performed regularly at Tyler's. "I only remember one club owner who really seemed to have figured out how to book modern jazz across—and keep a club going across the week," Marsalis later remarked.

> He didn't do it every night. It's a guy named [Fred] Laredo. He had a club on Magazine Street called Tyler's Beer Garden. I used to work on

> Wednesday nights with a bass player—wonderful young bass player at the time—named Reginald Veal, and a drummer named Noel Kendrick, who had gone to New Orleans Center for Creative Arts. We used to also—we'd back a singer from here, Germaine Bazzle. Every night Victor Goines used to come and sit in with us. So that worked fine, because on the weekends he [Laredo] would have—Friday, Saturday, Sunday—James Rivers Movement, which is a tenor saxophone player, rhythm-and-blues cat. He was a good saxophone player, but he played more. You couldn't even get in there. Them college kids was like that on Friday, Saturday, and Sunday. There were people who came to hear us on Wednesday, but it wasn't like we were trying to replace anybody. He understood all that. That's what the difference was, trying to look at the terrain and deal with the situation the way it is, and then place people in the spots that they need to be in.[17]

James Rivers—who lives on Constance Street, just around the corner from the club—played weekends there for a decade or so. During that time, many celebrities could be seen in the nightclub. One was Clint Eastwood, who hired Rivers to do soundtrack work on two of his films—including the acclaimed bio of Charlie Parker, *Bird*. Among the many other musicians who performed at Tyler's were Hector Gallardo and Caliente, saxophonist Red Tyler, pianist James Drew, and young, up-and-coming talents such as guitarist Steve Masakowski, bassist James Singleton, and drummer Johnny Vidacovich. Indeed, Astral Project was heard there regularly as well.[18]

The **Maple Leaf** on Oak Street (Uptown) had a more eclectic program, but there was not infrequently some trad or brass-band music to be heard (usually just one night per week).

Finally, for the sake of completeness, we cannot overlook short riverboat cruises with live jazz in the city's harbor area. Several boats—the *President*, the *Natchez*, *Creole Queen*, etc.—offered that form of entertainment. Likewise, weekend festivals and open-air concerts of one kind or another in the French Market or Jackson Square also seemed to become more popular during the decade.

The **Norwegian Seamen's Church** (NSC) on Prytania Street in the Lower Garden District (Uptown) continued to offer enough traditional jazz performances to warrant its sobriquet as "the Jazz Church" in the city. Pastor Kjell Nyland and his family completed their tenure there in 1983 and were honored with a farewell concert by trumpeter Wallace Davenport, singer Aline White, pianist Olivia Cook, and young vocalist Lillian Boutte. George Buck and Nina Rimington (Buck) were married there in 1986—a service that the NSC has increasingly performed in the local jazz community. (Lillian Boutte was later married there as well, and there have been many more, including *OffBeat*'s Jan Ramsey and Joseph Irrera, and the author and his wife, Sharyn.)

In this connection, it should be noted that the ubiquitous Helen Arlt lived right across the street from the Seamen's Church for many years, and her regular reports in *The Second Line* almost always made reference to the many musical activities at the church. Although deeply devoted to a different faith, she became a virtual *ex officio* member of the NSC.[19]

JAZZFEST IN THE 1980S

The New Orleans Jazz and Heritage Festival continued to grow and was becoming *the place* to be for music fans from around the world on the last weekend of April and first weekend of May each year. It was no longer the cozy event with down-home friendliness that it had been in the early '70s. The sight of celebrities such as Bette Midler, Mel Gibson, or former President Jimmy Carter was not unusual. Likewise, the late CBS News personality and *60 Minutes* correspondent Ed Bradley (1941–2006) was an annual visitor and clearly a keen fan of the sounds of (especially modern) jazz. By mid-decade, when more careful records had begun to be kept, attendance for the six-day event reached 250,000, and it had topped 300,00 by the end of the decade.

JazzFest was then presented by the non-profit New Orleans Jazz & Heritage Foundation, Inc., a Louisiana corporation under the supervision of a diverse board of directors. Locals Quint Davis, producer and director, and his erstwhile associate Allison Miner (Kaslow)—with the help and advice of many others—continued to line up the talent and serve as general managers of the festival. The overall format reverted to two weekends from 1980 onward. New stages were added, maybe most notable being the appearance of the Economy Hall tent in 1983. It served as the headquarters for traditional New Orleans jazz and its many fans, including countless dancers and second-liners. The other stage, which had in the past been devoted to both trad and modern jazz, was called simply the "Jazz Tent." Ultimately, it retained that name (though temporarily called the "Festival Tent") but then focused on the more modern idioms. (In the long term, jazz could be heard, at least in part, at other stages as well.) The total number of stages reached eleven by the festival's twentieth anniversary in 1989. The 1987 crowd of 300,000 at the Fair Grounds was said to have been the largest ever.[20]

As in the past, most of the headliners appeared in the evening concerts. They were frequently held on the steamboat *President* until it moved on (permanently) to St. Louis after the 1988 festival. A variety of spacious land venues such as the Municipal Auditorium and the Saenger Theatre on Canal Street served as alternate sites.

Some of the big jazz names to perform at JazzFest during the decade included Chick Corea, Flora Purim, Bob Crosby and the Bobcats, Betty Carter, Dorothy Donegan, Ramsey Lewis, Dexter Gordon, the Woody Herman Band, Gato Barbieri, Sonny Stitt, Cedar Walton, Jon Hendricks, Bobby McFerrin (with Astral Project), Oscar Peterson, Herbie Hancock, Elvin Jones, Carmen McRae, Herbie Mann, Miles Davis, Wynton Marsalis, Sarah Vaughan, Michael Brecker, Nina Simone, Jon Faddis, Celia Cruz, and Tito Puente. As always, the best of the local artists and bands were also represented.

Among the more popular draws were Jimmy Buffett, B. B. King, Taj Mahal, James Brown, Chuck Berry, Fats Domino, Dr. John, Ray Charles, Ry Cooder, Natalie Cole, the Neville Brothers, and Kenny G, as well as dozens of local groups.

One of the most talented musical visitors to the city during the decade was pianist **Tom McDermott**, who came to New Orleans for a gig at the World's Fair in 1984. He has called the Crescent City home ever since. A St. Louisan (like a number of other top New Orleans musicians) and a music graduate of Washington University, Tom is a first-class ragtime pianist as well as a knowledgeable student of all traditional piano styles (not to mention his deep devotion to the inimitable James Booker), an experienced writer, artist, and a gifted composer. Since establishing himself in the city, he has been a bandleader (with his Jazz Hellions), a co-founder of the popular New Orleans Nightcrawlers Brass Band, and a leader in the revival and local interest in an early Brazilian musical genre known as *choro*. He has also played and recorded with many local bands, including a five-year stint with the penultimate incarnation of the Dukes of Dixieland led by drummer Richard "Dickie" Taylor (1940–2010).

While McDermott is one of my personal New Orleans musical favorites, I bring up his name to recount a highly amusing and, at the same time, somewhat sobering commentary on JazzFest policies at the time. It will be a bare-bones account, but the bottom line should be quite clear.

After having been in town for a few years and having been rejected by JazzFest bookers six out of seven times, he concocted an audacious but quite elegant plan to change his "luck." He created a fictional blues pianist whom he called Clarence "Buckwater" Washington with "legendary" credentials. He then created the music for a tape that he called *Clarence "Buckwater" Washington: Live and Kickin'*, which he submitted to those who book the festival. He also submitted a cassette of his own music, under his own name, which, he noted, "anyone with a shred of musicality would see was far superior to Clarence's." But, as fate would have it, Buckwater was accepted and Tom was rejected once again. He later cancelled Buckwater's application.

McDermott told the story in full detail later on, but it doesn't take a rocket scientist to arrive at the bottom-line implication, sad but true as it may be. Tom summed up his account as follows: "Clarence 'Buckwater' Washington won't change things around here, but at least he brought a lot of happiness to guys I respect, both black and white."[21]

The festival had begun to receive criticism once again from a variety of sources for a variety of concerns, and, as the twentieth anniversary of the event approached, Quint Davis found it necessary to address *some* of that criticism with a letter to the editor of the *Times-Picayune*.[22] Among his comments therein, he noted, "The 1989 Jazz & Heritage Festival has contracted with 380 Louisiana groups to perform at the Heritage Fair at the Fair Grounds Race Track. The festival will employ approximately 5,000 Louisiana musicians, the most local talent of any music festival I know of in the world." He went on to conclude, "It is . . . the 20th time since George Wein came to New Orleans in 1970 with the vision of a unique New Orleans cultural celebration and created the New Orleans Jazz & Heritage Festival. Nothing in the history of the American music industry has done more to promote New Orleans music." There surely is much truth in that statement.

THE DEBUT OF THE FRENCH QUARTER FESTIVAL

One of the city's most popular and beloved annual musical events of the springtime (normally the second weekend in April, always two weeks prior to JazzFest) is the French Quarter Festival. It began in 1984 as something of a sequel to the "World's Fair" and was intended by Mayor Dutch Morial to be a mechanism to bring local residents back to the Quarter. The music was—and still is—entirely free and open to the public and features most of the same local (and even foreign) bands that appear at JazzFest. In fact, at least initially, it provided the intimate and friendly "reunion" atmosphere that had characterized the early years of the NOJ&HF.

It seems that, at the outset, funding for the FQF was provided largely by the city of New Orleans, but that is no longer the case. Indeed, there is now no municipal funding whatsoever. The main sources of support have come from sponsorships, along with beverage and merchandise sales. Like JazzFest posters, FQF posters have become very popular and have become rather valuable collectibles.

The focus for the music has always been open-air stages dispersed along Bourbon Street at intervals of about every other block. But additional stages were located on Royal Street and in Jackson Square. Eventually, the area along the river known as Woldenberg Park was incorporated into the festival grounds. (As of 2012, some twenty stages featured music ranging from jazz to classical and pop to international.)

While many jazz fans come from abroad to attend the activities—I know a number of Europeans, for example, who come to town to attend *only* the FQF—the event has always been especially popular among *local* festival-goers. In fact, if one would ask them, I am sure a majority would say that they prefer the French Quarter Festival to JazzFest by a considerable margin.

As a free event, FQF attendance cannot be easily estimated. Starting from an initial estimate of 50,000, the FQF has grown dramatically since its inception. The umbrella organization is now known as the "French Quarter Festivals, Inc.," and sponsors not only FQF but two additional events, the very popular "Satchmo SummerFest" and "Christmas New Orleans Style."

The growth and popularity of the French Quarter Festival are due in large measure to the first—and only—executive director, **Sandra Dartus**, for its first twenty years in business. A New Orleans native, the highly respected Ms. Dartus retired after SatchFest in August 2003 and moved to Wyoming with her new husband. But it is not uncommon to see her around town at key jazz events (including the FQF) to this day. While Dartus oversaw the growth of the festival, we cannot overlook the longtime and very significant contributions made to its musical programs year after year by her colleagues Eddie Bayard, Connie Jones, Ronnie Kole, and Don Marquis. In addition, the festival is now said to have the help of more than 1,500 community volunteers as well.[23]

The economic impact of FQF—like JazzFest—has been tremendously important to the city of New Orleans. And again, like JazzFest, the local cuisine helps to make the festival a success—to the extent that it bills itself as "the World's Largest Jazz Brunch." There can be little doubt but that JazzFest and FQF have inspired the creation of an almost endless number of other music festivals throughout the year that make New Orleans known world-wide as a festival town.

JAZZ EDUCATION IN THE 1980S

Turning once again to the New Orleans Center for Creative Arts (NOCCA), the jazz program directed by Ellis Marsalis since 1975 continued to produce outstanding graduates in the 1980s. A selection of alumni and former students from NOCCA's first decade or so includes trumpeter and composer Terence Blanchard; pianist-vocalist-actor Harry Connick Jr.; saxophonist Donald Harrison Jr.; bassist Elton Heron; choral composer and director Moses Hogan; flutist Kent Jordan; trumpeter Marlon Jordan; saxophonist Branford, trombonist Delfeayo, and trumpeter Wynton Marsalis; bassist Chris Severin; trumpeter Jamil Sharif; and drummer Stanley Stephens.

Describing some of the advantages of the breadth of the NOCCA program, 1983 grad Delfeayo Marsalis says, "In our performance classes, we would all perform for each other. So you might hear something from a Puccini opera. Then you might hear a Beethoven piano concerto. Then you'd hear *I Can't Get Started*. Then you'd hear *Now's the Time*. It was such a wide range of music, it gave us an appreciation for the relationship between the different styles."[24]

But Ellis Marsalis, who had also been a part-time member of the Loyola University music faculty since 1983, seems to have become somewhat disenchanted with the NOCCA jazz program by 1986. After twelve years in that capacity, he decided to leave for what appeared to him to be a more promising opportunity at Virginia Commonwealth University in Richmond, where he had been invited to become the founding director of a new jazz studies program. "At the time he left [New Orleans], Marsalis said that his classes at NOCCA had dwindled precipitously and that he was disheartened by the city's lack of interest in jazz."[25]

In a 1989 interview, Wynton Marsalis added, "In his [father's] jazz class at NOCCA, there were only five students: me, Branford, Terence Blanchard, Donald Harrison, Tony Dylan. When my father left the New Orleans Center for the Creative Arts, there were only three students [in his class]. So there is no New Orleans jazz school. It's only a media creation."[26]

Ellis Marsalis himself attempted to clarify those statements somewhat later:

> The 12 years that I spent at the New Orleans Center for Creative Arts, I don't want to say that I was bitter, because I wasn't, but I realized during those 12 years that the whole thing of talent is misconstrued

> by most people. I don't necessarily mean coming up with a definition of it. I saw so many kids who came through and had serious talent. They either fell by the wayside with some drugs or—not a lot of them did that though, I'd say—but most of them, music wasn't reinforced enough, I think, in their personal life. That's conjecture on my part, because you only get to know students so well for so long, and you never really know.
>
> Contrary to that, when you get the kind of support, especially parental support, which you get as a kid with a lot of talent, both parents are very supportive of him, then you get a Harry Connick, Jr. His parents are very supportive. His daddy was a D.A. His mother was a judge. She passed early in his life. When you get a situation like that, where somebody really has the talent and the support—but when you get to a point where you don't have the support, and there's some talent there, you're like swimming in syrup.[27]

If Marsalis had become slightly burned out with the jazz situation in the city as well as at NOCCA, his successor, trumpeter **Clyde Kerr Jr.**, breathed a new spirit into the school's program. A graduate of Xavier University and a professional trumpet player, Kerr came from a long line of musicians. His father, a respected music teacher in the public school system, also led the Clyde Kerr Big Band. Known as something of a taskmaster, Clyde Jr. taught at NOCCA for sixteen years and turned out a passel of young men who would make their marks in the jazz profession in the '90s and later. Trumpeter Nicholas Payton; drummers Adonis Rose and Jason Marsalis; trumpeter Irvin Mayfield; trumpeter and trombonist Troy Andrews; and trumpeter Christian Scott were just some of his prize students. As one can tell from most of those names, their teacher also instilled in them a sense of the business side of jazz. Mayfield seems to be a particularly good example of that.[28]

Meanwhile, after three years building the jazz program at VCU—one of his distinguished graduates was New Orleans reedman Victor Goines (now director of jazz studies at Northwestern University)—Ellis Marsalis was lured back to his hometown.

The aim of Chancellor Gregory O'Brien of the University of New

Orleans was to found a "premier" degree-granting jazz program at that institution. So, Marsalis, then fifty-four, was named to a chair with a million-dollar endowment given in large part by the Louisiana Coca-Cola Bottling Co., Ltd., to accomplish that objective. Marsalis later added, amusingly, "Coca Cola funded a million-dollar chair," but "a bunch of people in this town thought that Coke gave me a million dollars. I won't even go there."[29]

"My plan is to try to establish a model program for the serious study of jazz music," Marsalis said. "I want to create a training ground that will help establish a pool of musicians in the city. The point is, there's hardly any jazz musicians around New Orleans. There's older guys—people my age—but the young people have been leaving town or doing something else."[30] The new program began attracting promising young students from all over almost immediately.

As Jason Marsalis later recalled, "in '89 my father started a program at the University of New Orleans, and a whole flux of students came to New Orleans to study with him. There's piano players, like Glen Patscha and David Morgan. There's a wonderful trumpet player named Jeremy Davenport who came in. There's a bassist named Chris Thomas who came in. There's a drummer, Geoff Clapp. There was all these students that came into town. Brice Winston, the tenor saxophonist who now plays with Terence Blanchard. . . . It was a short time after that where there was a drummer who was going to Loyola at the time, but eventually he went to UNO. His name was Brian Blade. . . . and I was jealous of Brian—because folks—everybody—loved Brian's playing. Everybody used him."[31]

Many more impressive names could now be added to that list. Certainly some of them have remained in town and established their careers here, but others—like some of those to whom Marsalis was referring—have chosen to move to greener pastures after getting their start here. Yet, it seems pretty clear that the million-dollar investment has paid off handsomely for the university's image.

One of Marsalis's first faculty appointments was **Harold Battiste**, who was awarded a tenure-track position. Battiste later recalled:

> I was at UNO because Ellis invited me. . . . I got the feeling that the music department was not unanimous in the decision to introduce the students to jazz. I felt as though the jazz studies program was perceived by some other members of the music faculty to be harmful to the reputation of the department. But there we were in New Orleans, with all the many jazz resources that originated in the city. In my mind, a jazz education program based in New Orleans was like a perfect storm—all of the right elements were here and had been here for a very long time. This is music's epicenter, a cultural ground zero—I could really get carried away. Yet the controversy became an issue that merited a few faculty meetings with the department chair [Dr. Jeff Cox]. It was decided that we would have two divisions, classical and jazz, with some rules and regulations to manage the situation until some curriculum issues could be worked out.[32]

This was a situation that was not unique to this college jazz program.

Loyola University's jazz studies program in the College of Music and Fine Arts continued to grow under the supervision of **John Mahoney**, a fine trombonist, pianist, composer, and arranger. Mahoney had arrived at Loyola in 1978 after completing an M.M. degree from the Eastman School of Music. Joseph Hebert remained in charge of the jazz band until 1985, at which point Mahoney took over that responsibility. The Loyola University Jazz Band, directed by Mahoney, has received numerous honors and has been recognized for outstanding performances at a number of university jazz festivals. He also leads a first-rate big band in the city that does not get the kind of attention it deserves. Among the program's many notable alumni are Ellis Marsalis (M.M.), saxophonists Rick Margitza and Tony Dagradi (the latter now professor of saxophone at his alma mater), trombonist Antonio Garcia (head of the jazz studies program at Virginia Commonwealth University), and bassists Chuck Bergeron (on the University of Miami faculty) and Jesse Boyd (an adjunct member of the Loyola faculty).[33]

Recognizing the increasing need for jazz musicians to be aware of the business side of their art, Loyola University inaugurated a music industry studies program in the School of Music and Fine Arts in 1985. Joseph Hebert served as the program's first chair. Dr. Scott Fredrickson was later brought in from outside the existing faculty to head up the program, which offers both bachelor of music and bachelor of science degrees in music industry studies. This interdisciplinary program has continued to grow since that time.

Mention should be made of well-known avant-garde saxophonist **Edward "Kidd" Jordan**, who taught on the New Orleans campus of Southern University (SUNO) from 1974 until he retired at the age of seventy in 2005. A number of local African American musicians studied with Jordan, but, according to the mentor himself, there never was a formal jazz program at SUNO. As he put it, "I was a one-man show."[34] Among his students were trombonist Charles Joseph and baritone saxophonist Roger Lewis of the Dirty Dozen Brass Band, clarinetist Joe Torregano, trumpeters John Longo and Wendell Brunious, pianist Richard Knox, saxophonists Fred Shepherd and Reggie Houston, and on and on. It seems that such jazz offerings as were available when Jordan was a member of the faculty came to an end with his retirement. But Jordan, who now says, "I've always been a teacher," continues to this day to be deeply involved in local jazz education, especially with children.

The flagship campus of Southern University is in Baton Rouge, where famed avant-garde clarinetist **Alvin Batiste**, a product of the New Orleans public schools and a close friend of Jordan since they met as students at Southern in 1952, helped to found the influential Southern University Jazz Institute in 1969. He taught there for thirty-five years, during which time he produced an impressive list of jazz graduates. His former students include pianist/vocalist Henry Butler; bassists Roland Guerin, Chris Severin, and Reginald Veal; drummers Troy Davis, Herlin Riley, and Herman Jackson; saxophonists Branford Marsalis, Donald Harrison Jr., and Wess Anderson; flutist Kent Jordan; and trumpeter Maurice Brown, to name but a few. Batiste also became one of the country's first jazz artists-in-residence when the National Endowment for the Arts funded that program for three years in the New Orleans public schools from 1972 to 1974.[35] In order to carry out that assignment, he had the tedious task of commuting daily between Baton Rouge and New Orleans.

Alvin Batiste was probably at his artistic peak in the 1980s. He made a number of recordings in that decade, among which were three albums with "Clarinet Summit," a quartet that included other nationally notable clarinetists: John Carter, Jimmy Hamilton, and David Murray. Batiste passed away on May 6, 2007, at the age of seventy-five.

THE NEO–BRASS BANDS

While the traditional brass bands continued to have a significant role to play, in the African American community in particular, the "revolution" that Michael White had attributed to the later 1970s began to explode in the 1980s. It was an innovative movement that was directed to and embraced largely by a generation younger than the more senior jazz fans.

The **Dirty Dozen Brass Band**, which had gotten its start in the later '70s, hit the big time in the '80s—both at home and abroad. They made their first international tour in 1982 (Groningen, the Netherlands), followed two years later by a tour to Spain, France, and Italy (Umbria Jazz Festival in Perugia) organized by George Wein. In 1985, they played the Kool Jazz Festival in New York City, and they also played clubs in that city like the Village Gate.

Their first album, *My Feet Can't Fail Me Now* (a neo–brass band anthem), was also released in 1985. So, they were off and running. As trumpeter Greg Davis put it, "It was happening real fast."[36] And their popularity here and abroad remains to this day, with many of the core members of the original band (for example, Davis, Efrem Towns, Roger Lewis, Kevin Harris, Kirk Joseph) still very much engaged.

But the hot *new* band in the 1980s was the **ReBirth** (more commonly **Rebirth) Brass Band**, which was born in 1983.[37] It was founded by a triumvirate of teenagers, the Frazier brothers—Phil, sousaphone, and Keith, bass drum—and trumpeter Kermit Ruffins, who became the leader. They were heavily influenced initially by the Dirty Dozen, and even took over the latter's old residency at the Glass House, on South Saratoga and Second streets, Uptown/Central City.[38]

Rebirth may have achieved recognition and a popular reputation even more quickly than the Dozen. They were soon making trips to festivals in Europe and secured a recording contract with Rounder Records. They ultimately (1992) left the Glass House and established themselves as one of the regulars at the Maple Leaf on Oak Street, Uptown.

The charismatic **Kermit Ruffins** stayed with the band for a decade. But, at the age of twenty-eight, he started his own group—the Barbecue Swingers—in 1993 and took up residency at Vaughan's Bar and Grill in the Upper Ninth Ward. He started playing there with his band on Thursday night, the first of December 1993, and played that Thursday night gig at Vaughan's for almost twenty years, through August 2013. Over that span of time Ruffins became one of the best known and most popular young musicians in the city.[39]

Like their model, the Dirty Dozen, the Rebirth inspired the formation of other similar groups. Countless other brass bands in the same general style have come into existence since the members frequently came and went, forming new bands with different names along the way. Along with rock, the music of the neo–brass bands, as I like to call them, has become perhaps the most popular musical genre for the younger generations in the city—and beyond.

SOME LOCAL LUMINARIES OF THE 1980S

While looking forward to 1989, Don Marquis wrote in his final editorial of the previous year, "What 1988 meant to me was the awareness of the importance of New Orleans Jazz in other parts of the world." He then went on to discuss a loan from the local jazz museum collection to an exhibit in Darmstadt, Germany. He concluded by noting, "The Ascona Switzerland Jazz Festival now features more New Orleans Jazz Bands and musicians than our own N.O. Jazz & Heritage Festival does."[40] That is a good indication of the growing popularity and resurgence throughout the world of New Orleans and New Orleans music during this decade.

Indeed, a growing number of *European* trad bands in particular have incorporated "New Orleans" in the names of their groups. A quick perusal of a European jazz periodical such as the Swiss monthly *Jazztime* would reveal band names such as "Bogalusa New Orleans Jazzband," "Bourbon Street Jazz Band," "New Orleans Hall Jazz Band," "New Orleans Stompers," "New Orleans Hot Shots," and on and on. All are European-based bands (here mostly from German-speaking Switzerland), and their connection to New Orleans is largely in name only.

New Orleans musicians were traveling far and wide throughout the world, and in so doing they brought fame to their hometown and its music. If I had to pick the one local name that was most closely identified with this decade it would be, without much hesitation, "Marsalis." In fact, the well-known jazz critic and historian Leonard Feather has gone so far as to say, "the eighties would go down in history as the *Marsalis decade*."[41] It would be very difficult for me to argue with that.

On the other hand, the follow-up question becomes: *Which Marsalis*? Would it be to, as the National Endowment for the Arts eventually did in 2010, give *cumulative* recognition to *all* musical family members with their Jazz Masters award? For me, that would have been premature in the 1980s since some of the younger members such as Jason had yet to reach true stardom. Or would it be the *pater familias*, **Ellis Marsalis**, some of whose many achievements and contributions have been outlined above?

Or would it be his oldest son, the very talented saxophonist **Branford Marsalis**? After graduating from NOCCA in 1978, he moved on to Southern University (where he studied briefly with Alvin Batiste and roomed with Donald Harrison Jr.) and completed his education by graduating from the prestigious Berklee College of Music in Boston. He then went on to perform with Diz, Miles, and Herbie Hancock, before becoming a founding member of Sting's new band following the breakup of the Police. Like his younger brother, Branford's chops allowed him to win acclaim as both a classical and jazz performer.

Or maybe it would be **Wynton Marsalis**, one year younger than his saxophone-playing sibling and Ellis's second son? After graduating from NOCCA, he moved to New York City to attend Juilliard in 1979, but before finishing up, was soon gigging with the big boys, such as Art Blakey and Herbie Hancock. Wynton was certainly the one who was on the lips of more jazz critics and fans than any of the others at the time because of his trumpet virtuosity and jazz chops. By the time he was twenty-one, his talent was recognized throughout the world, and he was named by the British *Jazz Journal International* "Musician of the Year" for 1982. And just two years later, at the age of twenty-three, he won *two* Grammys for *both* classical and jazz recordings—the first New Orleans musician to do so. Accordingly, New Orleans dedicated a "Wynton Marsalis Day" on May 2, 1989. He was (and continues to be) a very intelligent, well read, and opinionated person—on almost any subject. He has demonstrated, both in our city and throughout the country, a talent for jazz education with the young.

Yet, for me, it is difficult to make a choice among the three of them. I suppose, if I had to pick one, it would be Wynton. And I will stick with that. Indeed, it may have been he who actually brought the nation's (world's) attention to the Marsalis name more than any of the others. In short, like Feather, I have no doubt but that the decade of the 1980s belonged to the name Marsalis.

Yet it would be with some reservations that I would omit others from New Orleans who brought fame and recognition to the city in the 1980s. One name in particular is another NOCCA grad, **Harry Connick Jr.** Already a legend in his hometown from early childhood as a piano player, he was playing at JazzFest by the age of ten in 1977. He made his recording debut in the following year with the LP *Dixieland Plus*, on which he performed with New Orleans veterans Roy Liberto, PeeWee Spitelera, Jim Duggan, Placide Adams, and Freddie Kohlman. His solo album *Twenty*, which happened to be his age, was released on the Columbia label with some appropriate fanfare in 1987. Accordingly, he was soon off to New York and, at the age of twenty-one, he opened at the posh Algonquin Hotel's Oak Room, one of Manhattan's top cabarets, in January 1989—to rave reviews. A versatile pianist who could play in almost any jazz style, he is also a singer often compared to early Sinatra. Yet, despite these impressive credits, Harry Jr. was still some way from top-billing stardom in the 1980s. But it was soon to come.

Although musicians such as Wynton, Branford, and Connick Jr. moved away from the city, they are always trumpeting (no pun intended) the virtues of New Orleans as they travel about the world. Moreover, they constantly return to town and, especially after Katrina, did an endless amount of good for the city both here and from afar.

Others to bring positive notoriety to their hometown during this decade were, in the traditional field, **Eddie Bayard** and his **New Orleans Classic Jazz Orchestra**. The NOCJO was another repertory band, initially aimed at recreating the spirit of the old New Orleans Owls of the 1920s. Bayard put the band together in 1984, and they became an almost immediate success. Their first recording, *The Owls Hoot* (1986), helped them to secure a series of international tours—mostly sponsored by the U.S. State Department—that took them to the Far East, South Pacific, Middle East, and India and Pakistan, where they often introduced (through concerts and workshops) New Orleans and New Orleans jazz to the very receptive host-country nationals.

"They laid out the red carpet for us," Bayard recalls. "They loved the music. We had press conferences all the time, and they asked us about the music. We gave clinics at the music schools. We taught the military band some tunes and had them jamming with us and reading some of our charts one time. We gave a little concert and class with questions and answers to school kids in school another time." The accomplishments of this fine musical organization (which still continues to perform on special occasions) has been greatly under-appreciated in its own hometown.[42]

Bayard had a hand in helping another important band of this era get started, namely, **Banu Gibson and the New Orleans Hot Jazz**. The Gibson organization, always stocked with outstanding individual talents, began in the early 1980s and toured in this country extensively during that decade—thus bringing New Orleans music to a large and varied American audience. One local writer suggested that she and the band had "probably built more of an out-of-town reputation than an in-town one." She reacted, "When we're on the road we probably do more to help keep the image of New Orleans music alive almost as much as any other group, except for maybe the Preservation Hall band. I hope that what we do keeps saying that this music's still alive." She then goes on to say, when talking about traditional jazz bands, "It shouldn't be where you have to see somebody ancient. I run up against that problem a lot. When you say you're from New Orleans, and you're not black and very old, they assume you're not playing jazz. Somehow they're really hung up on the mystique of images."[43] In my opinion, the Gibson band did not reach its musical peak until the following decade, so we'll leave further discussion of it until the following chapter.

Finally, a note about a major discovery during the decade. In 1988, highly respected jazz historian and Louis Armstrong biographer Gary Giddins commissioned New Orleans music historian and author **Thaddeus "Tad" Jones** and local attorney William Abbott to come to terms with the issue of Armstrong's birth. The trumpeter himself had always maintained that he had been born on July 4, 1900, but there had been questions about that. The upshot of their research, in short, revealed that a baptismal record indicated that Armstrong was, in fact, born on August 4, 1901.[44]

Jones admitted to being "surprised" by the discovery, and many in the jazz community were unwilling to accept the new finding. Indeed, a number of local musicians along with a handful of authorities around the world continued to observe Armstrong's birth on July 4, to the extent that his hundredth birthday was celebrated on July 4, 2000, throughout much of the jazz world. Yet virtually all jazz historians now take the August date to be the correct one.[45] Unfortunately, Jones did not live to complete the book about the trumpeter's early life in New Orleans on which he had been working for some time. He passed away tragically on January 1, 2007, at the age of fifty-four. Nevertheless, his discovery had a profound effect on jazz history and the life of perhaps the music's greatest practitioner.

JAZZ AND THE LOCAL MEDIA

There were no periodicals that dealt exclusively with jazz in the city, with the exception of course of the NOJC's *The Second Line*, and that was pretty much confined to the coverage of traditional jazz. It did an excellent job of doing that, especially during the editorship of Don Marquis. As of this writing, unfortunately, The *Second Line* is languishing at best.

Yet the NOJC, also struggling financially, continues to have hopes for its revival.[46]

New Orleans Music, edited by Mike Hazeldine, was established in 1990. It succeeded an earlier publication known as *Footnote*. Published in the United Kingdom, it, too, confined its coverage to traditional New Orleans jazz. But *NOM* ceased to exist in the early 2000s and has not been replaced.

A weekly entertainment (including music) tabloid, *Lagniappe*, has been included with the Friday *Times-Picayune* since 1980, when the newspaper merged with the old *States-Item*. The concept seems to have originated with the latter newspaper in 1970. Its coverage includes club listings and covers all music genres, with occasional feature pieces.[47]

A monthly tabloid devoted entirely to music (including jazz) was *Wavelength*, which made its first appearance in January 1980. Edited by Connie Atkinson (now on the history faculty of the University of New Orleans), it ceased to be published for financial reasons in late 1991. It, too, contained club listings and brief pieces about local musicians by local writers.

Yet another monthly of a similar type is *OffBeat*. Published by Jan Ramsey, who is also editor-in-chief, it got its start in 1988. It has continued to grow over the years and is now a slick and widely read magazine. Again, however, it does not confine its coverage to jazz and seems to increasingly cater to a broader audience. Gradually, it expanded its coverage to include art, books, and food. In the mid-'90s Ramsey introduced the "Best of the Beat Awards," an annual feature that has also grown in stature. The awards, voted on by the public, cover scores of categories from best bands, best instrumentalists, and best vocalists to best radio stations—across the local musical spectrum. This magazine, "one of the world's longest-running jazz and roots music publications," celebrated its twenty-fifth anniversary in December 2012.[48]

Gambit (or *Gambit Weekly*) is another free weekly publication founded in the decade of the 1980s (precisely 1981). Its focus is much broader than any of the above, serving as something of an alternative newspaper. (Its political editor, Clancy DuBos, is a respected authority on local politics.) Jazz coverage plays a less significant role in its overall coverage, but its "Big Easy (Entertainment) Awards" were inaugurated in 1988 and must have served as something of a model for those of *OffBeat*. Both awards continue to be offered annually.

Mention should perhaps be made of another local "alternative" weekly that covered a variety of subjects, including the local music scene: *Figaro*. It lasted less than a decade, from 1972 until 1981.

Music magazines, like music clubs in this city, come and go. Those listed above have been the most substantial of the lot. But, clearly, many are not devoted exclusively to jazz—despite the importance of that music to the city and its history—and their circulation, apart from *OffBeat*, is very limited. In fact, the only national jazz periodicals that have paid more than passing attention to New Orleans were *Downbeat* (published in Chicago), when Charles Suhor was a regular contributor in the 1960s, and *The Mississippi Rag* (published in Minneapolis), when I was invited to become the New Orleans columnist in the mid-'90s.

In December 1980, Texans **Jerry Brock** and his brother Walter officially inaugurated a community-based public radio station—**WWOZ** (90.7 FM)—that was to become the leading jazz and roots radio outlet in the city (and today brings New Orleans music to the whole world via the internet). (The call letters are said to be an acronym for "Wonderful World of OZ.") The original station was located in the boonies just outside the city, then to the upstairs at Tipitina's, eventually moving to a building in Armstrong Park in 1985 and its license transferred to the New Orleans Jazz & Heritage Foundation, which continues to provide substantial support for all its activities. (The station subsequently relocated to the French Quarter after Katrina.) "We have different shows that appeal to different people. It's amazing to see how these programs really do a service to the community," Brock said in a late 1980s interview.[49]

Musical coverage is extensive, ranging from programs devoted to traditional and contemporary jazz to a variety of Louisiana and international musical genres. Among my favorite programs for the last several years are the Latin (mainly Cuban) and Brazilian music sessions that take up most of Saturday afternoons (while opera is on the local NPR station).

Mike Gourrier, who came to be known as "Mr. Jazz of New Orleans," covered the largely modern jazz world from 1982 until Katrina drove him to Richmond, Virginia (though he continues to return to his birthplace periodically to do a variety of jazz-related activities). Referring to that period, he wrote in 2005, "Even the toppling of our broadcast tower was just a bump in the road as we rose in stature and established ourselves as the local purveyor of more jazz than all the rest of the stations in the city combined. National honors started to be acquired by the 'Little Station that Could.'"[50]

Another early institution at 'OZ was Betty "Big Mama" Rankin (1918–1998), who had a popular trad jazz program on Saturday mornings from the station's inception until shortly before her death in February 1998. (Her son is jazz guitarist and Loyola faculty member John Rankin.) Controversial and opinionated bandleader Bob French (1938–2012) also had a popular show for many years until he was let go because of differences with another of the station's jocks (Tom Morgan). WWOZ regularly receives "best" billing in the annual *OffBeat* polls.

Brief mention must also be made of the other public radio station in the city, **WWNO** (89.9 FM), headquartered at the University of New Orleans. The local NPR outlet, it, too, has had regular jazz programming for many years. That has recently been expanded with twenty-four-hour jazz coverage on its high-definition channel (WWNO-3). Professional programmers Fred Kasten and now Jack Hopke have always attempted to include local jazz (both trad and mod) in their programs devoted to jazz. Both also regularly conduct (taped) interviews with musicians and other notables in the local jazz community.

Returning to Jerry Brock, he played an important role in the larger New Orleans music scene in the '80s and '90s. "I always tried to be behind the scenes and supportive of the music and the New Orleans culture," he says modestly.[51] He was very much involved in the neo–brass band movement and was responsible for producing a number of important recordings, such as the first by the Dirty Dozen Brass Band in 1980. "It wasn't released—I still have the master tapes. We did it solely so that we could have their music to play on the radio, and we played it continually." He also produced one of the early Rebirth Brass Band recordings and may be best known as one of the co-producers of the Grammy-winning Verve CD by Doc Cheatham and Nicholas Payton in the '90s.

Along with Barry Smith, he founded the renowned record emporium, the **Louisiana Music Factory**, in 1992. (Now totally under the control of Smith, it continues to be *the* shop for New Orleans music in the city.) Brock seems to have been somewhat less active in the music scene since Katrina, but he told me in 2008 that he had been commissioned to write a history of the legendary Monteleone Hotel in the French Quarter, said to be the second-oldest family-owned hotel in this country.

A FINAL LOOK AT THE 1980S

"New Orleans continues to be one of the big post-oil-and-gas-boom losers, a shoulda-woulda-coulda gambler, a place where the harsh light of insolvency makes the politicians' greed seem particularly obscene and their dreams of a mass-market tourist economy appear more threatening and pathetic than visionary. Times are tough here in the backwash of what we're told has been a time of solid-growth nationally. . . . Yet the music has rarely been so abundant or the players so driven by creative energy."[52] Such are the words of one (outside) observer at the end of the decade.

We have seen that, despite the economic woes of the gas and oil industry, the city experienced a number of music accomplishments in the 1980s. In addition to those outlined above, we might consider the following.

Massachusetts-based Rounder Records issued a three-LP set entitled *The New New Orleans Music* in 1988. Produced by New Orleanian Kalamu Ya Salaam and recorded over a two-year period, it featured a series of modern New Orleans musicians in a variety of jazz styles: "Jump Jazz," "Vocal Jazz," and "New Music Jazz." It was pretty clearly an attempt to follow up on Harold Battiste's AFO boxed set of '50s and '60s modern New Orleans jazz, and was, in fact, dedicated to him. Even a few from the earlier roster of musicians (for example, James Black, Ellis Marsalis, Red Tyler) reappeared in this set.

While, in my view, the quality of the music varies somewhat, there are many outstanding individuals involved, from veterans Marsalis, Ed Frank, Red Tyler, James Black, Earl Turbinton, Fred Kemp, Roger Lewis, and Kidd Jordan to relative youngsters like Kent Jordan, Tony Dagradi,

Wendell Brunious, Steve Masakowski, Herlin Riley, Victor Goines, and Reginald Veal. An impressive group, to be sure, and there are others as well. Altogether, it gives a sampling of the state of modern jazz in the city in the mid- to late 1980s.

The Rounder record label came to be increasingly interested in and committed to New Orleans music and musicians during the era. In fact, Scott Billington, the label's vice-president and A&R man, was given a Best of the Beat Award by *OffBeat* magazine in 2012.

These LPs were recorded between 1985 and 1987 at four different studios in the metropolitan area: Ultrasonic (Scott Goudeau, engineer) in New Orleans, Studio Solo (David Farrell, engineer) in nearby Slidell, Southlake Recording Studio (Farrell) in suburban Metairie, and Composers' Recording Studio (Goudeau) in New Orleans. Yet the editing and mastering were carried out in Massachusetts and New York. Ultrasonic Studio was a popular site for jazz recording sessions. Unfortunately, it was destroyed by the flooding of Katrina and never rebuilt.

Maybe the busiest jazz recording studio was that associated with George Buck's Jazzology Records (above the Palm Court Café on Decatur Street). Richard Bird has been the longtime engineer there. The Jazzology label is of course best known for its recordings of traditional jazz.

The jazz AFO label, which was established by Harold Battiste in 1961, fell into abeyance during his long period in Los Angeles. When he returned to New Orleans in 1989 to take up his post in the new jazz studies program at UNO, he began making plans to revive the label. That process did not begin until early in the following decade, when other new labels (both trad and mod) began to appear on the local scene.

On the subject of local record labels, to anticipate a bit, I will mention here Basin Street Records, which did not get under way until 1997. It began with a live recording of Kermit Ruffins and his Barbecue Swingers, just the first of a dozen projects for him with the label. Since then Basin Street has issued scores of albums by the likes of Dr. Michael White, Irvin Mayfield and Los Hombres Calientes, Jeremy Davenport, Henry Butler, Jason Marsalis, the Rebirth Brass Band, and many others. By the next century, it had become a major voice for the dissemination of New Orleans jazz.

I close this chapter with a quotation that I consider quite apropos from the distinguished historian and critic Gary Giddins.

> Then came the '80s, and suddenly jazz has a dose of New Orleans fever again. When Art Blakey showcased Wynton and Branford Marsalis, their backgrounds were of passing interest. But when he replaced them with two more New Orleanians, Terence Blanchard and Donald Harrison, and when rumor promised lots more where they came from, notably a flutist named Kent Jordan, the city began to loom once again in the imagination. Especially since each of these musicians was schooled in classical as well as jazz music—just like the Creoles of Color who set the standards for jazz musicianship at the turn of the century. . . . Ellis Marsalis hasn't unleashed an assemblage of geniuses, but rather a cadre of impeccably schooled musicians. Following them as they rise to the challenges that their abilities and backgrounds dictate will be one of the chief pleasures of jazz listening in the '80s.[53]

Amen.

Vaughan's Lounge was founded in 1981 and has since become associated with trumpeter Kermit Ruffins and his band.

Tyler's Beer Garden featured a host of modern jazz artists during the 1980s, here the young trio of David Torkanowsky, piano; James Singleton, bass; and Johnny Vidacovich, drums. *Photo courtesy of Fred Laredo.*

Fred Laredo at the door of the former Tyler's Beer Garden, which he ran so successfully, April 2012.

The Palm Court Jazz Café on Decatur Street opened in 1989. This photo illustrates the club's tenth anniversary.

George Buck in a familiar pose, at the telephone in his office above the Palm Court, 1997. The founder of Jazzology and GHB record labels, the sightless Mr. Buck could walk a short distance from his desk to shelves full of recordings and immediately pick out whatever it was that one was looking for.

Clarinetist Don Suhor is typical of so many fine New Orleans musicians. An outstanding modernist, he moves comfortably to the traditional style as well. He is seen here at the Palm Court Café in the 1990s. Bassist Dewey Sampson is in the background.

Two of the mainstays at Preservation Hall for decades were trumpeter Percy Humphrey and clarinetist Willie Humphrey, seen here in 1989, only a few years before they were no longer part of the New Orleans jazz scene. The pianist is Sadie Goodson Colar, but the bassist cannot be identified.

Among the many annual celebrity visitors to JazzFest were former President and Mrs. Jimmy Carter. Here they are seen enjoying the music in the Economy Hall Tent at JazzFest in 1997.

Edward "Kidd" Jordan, *right*, is the city's leading jazz avant-gardist and a respected jazz educator. He is seen here with one of the city's legendary traditionalists, trumpeter Alvin Alcorn, in this backstage photo at JazzFest 1997.

Harry Connick Jr.'s immense popularity is revealed by this 1989 view of the Jazz Tent where he was performing at JazzFest. The interior was filled to capacity, and we see the crowd gathered outside to catch a bit of his performance.

Bourbon Street during the French Quarter Festival in the 1980s. Note the band playing in the left foreground.

Eddie Bayard and the New Orleans Classic Jazz Orchestra at French Quarter Fest 1989. The band members are, *from left*, Kenny Hall, Tom Ebbert, Bayard, Jacques Gauthé, Amy Sharpe, and Steve Pistorius. The bassist is Jim Black.

Among the many European bands to appear at the Norwegian Seamen's Church, and one of the first, was the popular Ytre Suløens Jass-ensemble from Norway. Seen here is the YSJE's talented young trumpeter Kaare Nymark. In the background is clarinetist Jens Arne Molvaer, one of the band's co-founders.

Clyde Kerr Jr., *left,* and Ellis Marsalis may be discussing the jazz program at NOCCA in this photo. Each had a major hand in the development of the school's excellent reputation.

The late Alvin Batiste was an outstanding modern jazz clarinetist as well as a longtime jazz educator.

Kermit Ruffins may be the city's most popular musician today. The first leader of the Rebirth Brass Band in the 1980s, he started his Barbecue Swingers in 1993.

Henry Butler, Tom McDermott, and Jerry Brock, *left to right*, share a smile before Butler goes onstage at the Louisiana Music Factory in the early 1990s.

New Orleans celebrated its native son Wynton Marsalis with a day-long tribute on May 2, 1989. This banner flew above Royal Street in the French Quarter.

4

A "Golden Age" for Traditional Jazz?

THE 1990S

In the course of his discussion of a new recording by cornetist Chris Tyle, who had moved to New Orleans from the West Coast in 1989, jazz historian and critic Paige VanVorst wrote, "There was a lot of work during that period. In some respects it was a golden age for younger traditional jazz players. There were quite a few clubs featuring live music and a young player with the proper skills could work almost all the time during those days and there were always spot jobs and an active street music scene."[1]

There is much truth in that statement, as it pertains to the later 1980s and 1990s. Several musicians would say that there was much more work for them here than in much larger cities such as New York. Not surprisingly, then, a significant number of top-notch young musicians moved to town during the period to join an impressive group of local "young lions" who had begun to be recognized beyond the city itself. I would hasten to add, however, that these fine young players were not just playing traditional jazz. The influence of the Marsalis brothers and other young hot shots from the previous decade had a notable impact on the young musicians of the decade. (I will leave to others a discussion of a new sound—"rap"/"bounce"—that began to reverberate on the streets of the city in the early '90s.)

Under mayors Sidney Barthelemy (1986–94) and Marc Morial (1994–2002), the state of Louisiana experienced—with considerable (and justifiable) apprehension initially—the legalization of gambling in June 1992 and the official onset of legalized gambling by the end of 1993. After a stumbling/bumbling start, the splashy Harrah's Casino finally opened its doors in October 1999 on the site of the old Rivergate convention center at the foot of Canal Street.[2] That phenomenon surely served as an additional shot in the arm for the ever-growing tourist industry and, by extension, the local music scene. I have to say, however, that I never got the impression that the tourists drawn to town by gambling were much taken by jazz—despite Harrah's early efforts to offer some fine local jazz combos (both trad and mod) to the public. Indeed, the gambling crowd seemed more interested in the bars and T-shirt shops on Bourbon Street than the few remaining jazz clubs, which may help to explain the eventual shift away from "The Street" as a primary focus for jazz music.

A BRIEF OVERVIEW OF THE CLUB SCENE IN THE '90S

An unusually large number of veteran New Orleans jazz musicians, it seems to me, passed away during the 1990s. The list—doubtless incomplete—would include, in chronological order: reedman Charlie Cordilla, drummer Freddie Kohlman, pianist "Sing" Miller, trombonist Louis Nelson, and bassist Chester Zardis (all 1990); guitarist Justin Adams and reedman Eddie Miller (1991); drummer Ed Blackwell, bassist Sherwood Mangiapane, trumpeter Teddy Riley, and violinist-composer Bill Russell (1992); trumpeter Murphy Campo (1993); guitarist/banjoist Danny Barker, reedman Clarence Ford, and clarinetist Willie Humphrey (1994); trumpeter Percy Humphrey (1995); reedman "Pud" Brown, trumpeter Kid Sheik Colar, and trombonist Paul Crawford (1996); drummer Louis Barbarin (1997); pianist Ed Frank, and I would include non-native trumpeter Doc Cheatham, who made such a positive impact on the city's jazz scene during this decade (1997); singer "Blue Lu" Barker, trombonist Homer Eugene, bassist James Prevost, and drummer Phil Zito (1998); trumpeter Jimmy Ille and clarinetist Tony Mitchell (1999).

The loss of these stalwarts clearly had an impact on the local club scene, particularly at **Preservation Hall.** Nevertheless, there were plenty of experienced younger players (like trumpeter John "Kid" Simmons; the Brunious brothers, trumpeters John and Wendell; and pianist John Royen) to fill most of the voids—in addition to holdovers such as banjoist Narvin Kimball and trombonist Frank Demond. Preservation Hall continued to be the first stop for many jazz fans visiting the city from out of town.

The **Palm Court Jazz Café** was also affected by the losses. Danny Barker and Pud Brown were serious blows to their programming. Yet talented veterans like trumpeter Lionel Ferbos, trombonist Tom Ebbert (1919–2012), banjoist Les Muscutt, bassist Chuck Badie, and drummer Ernie Elly remained. And to them one might add relative youngsters like trumpeters Gregg Stafford (who took over Barker's Jazz Hounds) and Clive Wilson, clarinetist Brian O'Connell, pianist Lars Edegran, and trombonist Lucien Barbarin.

One of the characteristics of New Orleans jazz then and now has been the fluidity of the talent pool and the increasing absence of bands with permanent personnel. Jazz venues like the two just mentioned tried earnestly to pass the work around by using a variety of musicians in a somewhat balanced way. Some musicians objected to that policy.[3]

Maison Bourbon, the oldest continuously running Dixieland club on Bourbon Street, continued to play an important role with its unique afternoon and evening bands. Veteran trumpeters Roy Liberto and Wallace Davenport may have been the big draws. But some very good younger musicians like trumpeters Leroy Jones and Jamil Sharif (son of the great Umar Sharif/Big Emery Thompson) passed through those venerable portals as well. Indeed, I vividly remember seeing a wonderful group of twenty-somethings led by bassist Mitchell Player holding forth there late in the decade. The fine clarinetist Louis Ford (son of the great Clarence) was the "old man" of the group at the age of thirty-seven. All of these young men have gone on to greater things.

Several venues, both old and new, reached early peaks during this decade. One such was **Fritzel's** on Bourbon Street. In my opinion, this was due in large measure to the success of the weekly weekend jam sessions led by veteran clarinetist and bandleader Jack Maheu (a one-time member of the Dukes of Dixieland), who had only moved to town from the East Coast at the beginning of the decade. At Fritzel's, Maheu started out in a basic trio format with piano (David Boeddinghaus, John Royen, and Tom McDermott probably being the most frequently heard) and drums (Richard "Dickie" Taylor, when he was not leading the latest edition of the Dukes). Maheu later added a bass (Bernie Attridge and Everett Link, among many others). Cornetist Eddie Bayard often sat in after his afternoon gig on the steamboat *Natchez*. Likewise, later in the evening other musicians would flood in after their gigs were over: trumpeter Wallace Davenport, cornetist Chris Tyle, bandleader Banu Gibson, and many others. As a highly respected clarinetist, Maheu tended to draw younger clarinet players to his gigs, most notably Tim Laughlin, Tom Fischer, Brian Ogilvie, and Evan Christopher. All admitted to having profited from their working with Maheu. Other talented youngsters like trumpeter Duke Heitger and cornetist Scott Black also came in to learn from "the General," as Maheu came to be known by many of those young men. It was, in short, a lively and exciting environment that also attracted big (despite the tiny room) and enthusiastic crowds as well as visiting musicians.[4]

Another venue that also attracted visiting musicians along with large numbers of trad aficionados was the **Can Can Jazz Café** in the Royal Sonesta Hotel, also on Bourbon Street. Multi-instrumentalist Chris Tyle, who had arrived in the city just a few years earlier after playing with bands on the West Coast, led his Silver Leaf Jazz Band there for a decade starting in 1992. (The club closed soon after that gig concluded.) The personnel in his band varied over time, but it included, among others, pianists Tom Roberts and Steve Pistorius; reedmen Orange Kellin, Dan Levinson, and Jacques Gauthé (Tyle, a fine cornetist and drummer, even took up the clarinet and soprano sax during his stay at the Can Can); bassist Tom Saunders; and ace drummer Hal Smith. Many top local and visiting musicians sat in as well: trumpeter Duke Heitger; his father, Ray, a clarinet-playing bandleader from Ohio; and Duke's old buddy, cornetist Jon Erik Kellso from New York City being just a few of them. The Can Can was a major trad venue during its brief floruit.

Another major venue for traditional jazz that flourished for only a brief period at this time was located in the **Meridien Hotel** on Canal Street. The house band for much of its lifespan was Jacques Gauthé's Creole Rice Yerba Buena Jazz Band, an ensemble inspired by that of Lu Watters on the West Coast. It consisted initially of Gauthé on clarinet and soprano saxophone; Scott Black, cornet; Tom Ebbert, trombone; Amy Sharpe, banjo; Tom Saunders, bass; and Kenny Hall, drums. The pianists included John Royen and Tom McDermott. Gauthé, who was born and raised in France as a protégé of the legendary Sidney Bechet, often brought fellow French reedmen like Claude Luter and Maxim Saury to town as well as Bob Helm from the original West Coast band. Live jazz at the Meridien essentially disappeared by the end of the century, the hotel was closed, and it had been replaced by the J. W. Marriott as of this writing.

A venue that I had great hopes for was **Storyville District** (not to be confused with the old Storyville Jazz Hall, 1104 Decatur Street). Located just off Canal Street at 125 Bourbon Street, it (officially) opened with a splash on January 7, 1999. (There had been a preliminary opening in December 1998.) It contained two main music rooms, a larger and a smaller. The latter, known as "The Parlor," struck me as the prototypical jazz room—both in terms of its attractiveness and its intimacy. Initially, the club featured both quality trad and contemporary jazz in the afternoon as well as the evening. Eventually, owner Quint Davis (of JazzFest fame) was unable to keep the club going at the high standard he sought—so he sold it to an out-of-town group that immediately turned it into a tasteless pop-music club.

Another short-lived club nearby was **Levon Helm's Classic American Café**, 300 Decatur Street. A press release announced its opening as follows: "In what many are calling the most important entertainment development in New Orleans since House of Blues, Tony Mart Orleans, LLC, announced the December 26, 1998, Grand Opening of 'Levon Helm's Classic American Café,' a live music supper club. . . . In addition to THE BAND's legendary drummer, Levon Helm, the club will count among its partners New Orleans' own Banu Gibson, internationally acclaimed jazz, blues and swing songstress. Grand Opening celebrations will include special performances by Levon, Banu, the Staple Singers, James Cotton, and numerous friends and guest stars including THE BAND." At the time of the opening of his club, Helm seems to have already been suffering from cancer (which ultimately took his life in 2012)—but the day-to-day management of the place was in the hands of one Carmen

Marotta. Unfortunately, Helm's New Orleans venture had already failed long before his death.

I was out of the country for Banu's real opening in January 1999, which also included Al Belletto's big band. She labeled it "an incredible success," adding, "And the swing dancers came in for the second half of it. They were dancing up a storm. It was very nice to see people actually touching while they danced, again. We're back to that."

But, by the time I caught her gig later in January, Marotta was already expressing (to me) his concerns about the turnouts at the venue. Later that night, I asked Banu herself about how the club was doing, and she replied, "It's growing pains. It's just like your newborn, starting to walk. It stands and falls, stands and falls. But I hear really good things from everybody that comes in. I think it's got the potential to be a permanent, wonderful home." And when asked about being a club owner, she said, "Well, it's going to be harder to fire me, isn't it? I like it. It's fun." Unfortunately, it was soon over. The club closed its doors for good in mid-May, less than six months after opening. It had been her many fans' hope (as well as her own) that it would serve as her home base in New Orleans for years to come.

Gibson and her band had had a short time earlier a brief stand at another nearby, upper Bourbon Street (#216) club. **Swing Town** opened in January 1997, seemingly with the idea of profiting from the popularity of the swing-dance craze. (Its musical director was bandleader Johnny Angel, who fancied himself as the local swing-dance leader.) It was an attractive and quite large room, but it was soon apparent that the (surly) management didn't have a clue about swing music (or much else musically). Nevertheless, Banu's band appeared there on a fairly regular basis for a couple of months—she said that she even offered to lease the place—but it soon died, being turned into a go-cup daiquiri club without live music. The whole thing turned out to be just another example of a wasted opportunity, due largely to funding deficiencies and mismanagement.

I'll not say more about other abortive efforts to start clubs in the French Quarter during this decade. Yet, one point seems clear. The fact that a number of people envisioned a need for more jazz clubs suggests that they perceived sufficient public interest for such ventures. It was an optimistic time.

Turning to the periphery of the Quarter, there were many knowledgeable people who believed that North Rampart Street would replace Bourbon Street and become the future home of jazz in the city. Musician Jack Maheu was one of them. When asked about the future of jazz in New Orleans in a mid-'90s interview, he said, "I predict that the next two jazz centers in New Orleans will be on Frenchmen Street and Rampart Street. I think Bourbon Street is pretty much washed up, except for a few lonely outposts of jazz. It will take a while, but it will probably go the way that Times Square did. They outpriced themselves."[5] As it has turned out, his predictions were remarkably prescient. And, indeed, he made several abortive attempts to line up a site for his own club on North Rampart.

But opening music clubs across from Armstrong Park has a history of problems with the neighborhood and the city council. Nevertheless, one venue that managed to overcome those obstacles was **Donna's Bar & Grill**, at the corner of Rampart and St. Ann. The club was started by Donna Poniatowski, a school teacher, and her husband, Charlie Sims, a retired Amtrak chef, in October 1993. It had come to be known as the city's "brass band headquarters," but it should be noted that the musical programming was more eclectic than that and included a good bit of jazz by the likes of Bob French, Irvin Mayfield, Leon Brown, Leroy Jones, Tom McDermott, Evan Christopher, and others. Poniatowski even made a foray into the recording business, starting a record label known as Rampart Records. Their first recording, by a Madison, Wisconsin, brass band (Mama Digdown's Brass Junction), was released in January 1999. Poniatowski and Sims eventually closed the club and moved to Florida, and efforts to reopen it were rebuffed by city government.[6]

About a block up the street from Donna's was another club, the **Funky Butt (at Congo Square)**, 714 N. Rampart (Rampart at St. Peter), just across the street from Armstrong Park. Its proprietor, the idiosyncratic Richard Rochester, said he was inspired by his friend Danny Barker (who had died just two years earlier) to open a music club cum restaurant. Accordingly, the venue was inaugurated in April 1996, just in time for JazzFest. Its upstairs music hall was dubbed "The Danny Barker Room."

The music itself varied from trad to mod jazz and brass-band styles. The opening night featured pianist Henry Butler and the Li'l Rascals Brass Band, with saxophonist Donald Harrison Jr. and the Newbirth Brass Band the next evening. Among others to appear at the Butt were trumpeter Irvin Mayfield, trombonist Delfeayo Marsalis, and pianist Victor Atkins. Rochester sold his interest in the club and moved out of town shortly before Katrina hit. Again, efforts to reopen it were thwarted by the city council.

OffBeat editor-publisher Jan Ramsey opined later, "Music may never again be heard on North Rampart Street, unless it's from the occasional festival that takes place in Armstrong Park." (As of this writing, the latter looks better than ever. As the headquarters of the Jazz National Historical Park, it should be the home of many lively music performances beyond merely festivals.) Ramsey concludes, "North Rampart Street's development has been pathetic—despite the fact that it was not severely damaged by the hurricane. But that's because it's in a stranglehold of stunted development, controlled by a small group of residents who don't want a commercial street. They only want residential properties, or galleries, or restaurants (none of which has taken off)."[7]

Finally, Jack Maheu's prediction above was at least spot on with respect to Frenchmen Street, though Snug Harbor's George Brumat still considered the musical neighborhood as a "work in progress" at the time.[8]

Snug Harbor on Frenchmen Street continued to be the main contemporary jazz club in the city, as it had been for much of the previous decade. It featured the music of pianist Ellis Marsalis on a regular basis and attempted to showcase top local bands such as Astral Project and all other locals who were into contemporary jazz, but it also brought in national and international "name" talent such as reedmen Steve Lacy or Eddie Harris from time to time. It was clearly *the* place to go to hear good modern jazz in the city.

Another club usually featuring modern jazz opened in September 1999. **Sweet Lorraine's**, 1931 St. Claude Avenue, was formerly known as "Lorraine's Dugout." Newly renovated as both eatery and music venue, the new club quickly came to be a popular hangout for modern-jazz enthusiasts. People who performed there early on included singer

Germaine Bazzle, singer-bassist George French, singer Phillip Manuel, singer Wanda Rouzan, singer Kim Prevost and her guitar-playing husband Bill Solley, pianist Henry Butler, saxophonist James Rivers, and young trumpeter Nick Payton—among others. The club continues in business and is doing well to the time of this writing.

The relatively short-lived Louisiana Jazz Federation (LJF) was flourishing in the mid-'90s, and it was they who dubbed October "Jazz Awareness Month" in the city. To celebrate, they inaugurated a series of free Sunday afternoon concert-dances at **Café Brasil**, on the corner of Frenchmen and Chartres, in October 1994. The music for these occasions was almost always traditional jazz and featured some of the top bands in town, even though the venue itself was known for a more eclectic musical fare.

The concept of a month devoted to an emphasis on jazz ran contrary to the national designation of April, but the LJF's decision was based on October being a musically slower month than April. So, the official christening of Jazz Awareness Month took place on October 2, 1994, with a concert-dance featuring the band of Percy Humphrey. The event was so successful that it was repeated in the following year and officially dubbed (in accordance with a venerable tradition) "Nickel-A-Dance." In 1996, Nickel-A-Dance became a series of "soirees" (4:00–7:00 p.m.) with a different band each Sunday during the month. All of these occasions were held at Café Brasil through the end of the decade. The series has continued to exist and grow in popularity to the present day, but the concept of "jazz awareness" seems to have disappeared with the end of the LJF (officially, soon after the turn of the millennium).[9]

The **Dream Palace**, 534 Frenchmen, remained in place with a diverse musical menu, but its name would change several times in the next few years. Its music tended to be geared, in large part, to the younger generation. But the New Leviathan Orchestra played the occasional Sunday afternoon "tea dance" there.

It wasn't until the next decade that Frenchmen Street would explode and become something of a successor to Bourbon Street, when Snug's Jason Patterson would say, "It would be nice to stretch [the street's musical action] all the way to St. Claude Avenue—all the way to Sweet Lorraine's."[10]

FRENCH QUARTER FESTIVAL IN THE 1990S

Under the dedicated and tireless leadership of Sandra Dartus, the FQF continued its spatial and numerical growth during this decade. According to a 1997 press release, attendance—still difficult to determine with precision—attracted some 300,000 people (up substantially from the 50,000 attendees during the first year).

The press release goes on to note:

> In a survey of 1996 festival-goers by the University of New Orleans, 39.5% gave the [festival] a 10 rating, while 47% rated it 8 or 9. When asked to complete the sentence, "*French Quarter Festival is better than . . .*" 23% responded "*Jazz Fest*" and 21% said "*Mardi Gras.*" Results also indicated that more than 41% of those surveyed came from outside New Orleans; 58% live within the area—thus, the goal of bringing locals back to the Quarter is working hand in hand with tourism efforts. A similar survey several years earlier projected the economic impact of the event to be nearly $10 million.

I would guess that the results of the polling were on the conservative side.

An October 1996 press release indicated that FQF fans "come in from England, Germany, France and the Netherlands, as well as throughout the U.S." I have friends who come every year from Norway and Switzerland. And, by the end of the decade, an "international stage" had been added on Bourbon Street, with bands from Australia, Austria, Canada, the United Kingdom, and so on. Some of these and other foreign jazz bands would also appear at **Fritzel's** and the **Norwegian Seamen's Church**. As always, the latter had a rich menu of jazz bands during the FQF and JazzFest weeks. As Dartus noted, these foreign visitors "love our music and often comment that French Quarter Festival is the best showcase for real, New Orleans jazz."

In 1999, an ancillary event—not officially part of FQF but held on the Friday and Saturday of the festival—was the "Duke Ellington Centennial Colloquium: Researching New Orleans Music." The keynote address was given by John Hasse, curator of American music at the Smithsonian

Institution in Washington, D.C. His 1993 book on Ellington had been very well received. Hasse's address was followed by many other fine presentations by local authorities such as Bruce Raeburn, Michael White, and Jack Stewart. Obviously, the emphasis was on the Ellington–New Orleans connections, of which there are many.

The Ellington colloquium was the third in an annual series known as the "International Music Colloquium," but held for the first time in connection with the FQF. Colloquium coordinator Dr. Connie Atkinson of UNO called this event a dream come true. "For ages," she explained, "several of us who research New Orleans music . . . have talked about some way that we could get together and share our information and research methods. Three years ago, we celebrated Bechet's birthday with a small colloquium on Bechet [post-JazzFest]. Last year we held the colloquium at Loyola University and discussed jazz education. This year, I believe we've found a home with the French Quarter Festival. The theme of next year's colloquium will be New Orleans and the Caribbean, an area that many of us would like to know more about."

These gatherings may well have stimulated the ultimate realization of the FQF's "Satchmo SummerFest," which debuted in August 2001.

JAZZFEST IN THE 1990S

The New Orleans Jazz and Heritage Festival continued its steady growth in attendance due in large part, in my opinion, to its efforts to appeal to as large an audience as possible—of which, we know all too well, jazz is only a very small component.

The 1990 edition did not have one of its best lineups. Nevertheless, we are told, "On May 6 [the second Sunday], public radio stations in 29 cities including Boston, Los Angeles, Washington, and Detroit broadcast six hours of the Jazz Fest live. Another 36 stations aired a delayed version. Some of the musicians covered were The Neville Brothers, Etta James, B. B. King, Gary Burton Reunion, Linda Ronstadt, Walter Hawkins, Zachary Richard and Flaco Jiménez. The broadcast was produced by WGBH radio in Boston with WWNO-FM and WWOZ-FM in New Orleans, WPFW-FM in Washington, DC and Murray Street Enterprises in New York City."[11]

In 1993, WWOZ started taping live performances at the festival. They began issuing these performances on CDs in a series called "The Sounds of New Orleans" as premiums during the station's semiannual fund-raising drives. Volume 2 (1994) in the series did the same but also included live performances from other occasions between the fall of '92 and the summer of '94, and that practice was followed in subsequent editions as well. The CDs in this series contained a lot of good jazz as well as live performances by a variety of other local groups.

A major fire totally destroyed the Fair Grounds grandstand in December 1993. It had a significant effect on JazzFest in subsequent years, especially after the eventual construction of a handsome new grandstand (in time for the 1998 fest) that allowed for many new features in the festival's program and amenities. In addition, Quint Davis noted in a January 1994 interview in *OffBeat*, "It's kind of ironic. For years we've discussed the option of expanding into the parking lot with tents. Now, out of the ashes of this catastrophe, it may happen."

The twenty-fifth anniversary festival, a seven-day event (April 22–May 1, 1994), included the following talent: Willie Nelson, Count Basie Orchestra, Taj Mahal, B. B. King, Etta James, Newport Allstars, Joshua Redman, Benny Powell, Little Richard, Frankie Ford, the Band, Jon Faddis, the Dixie Cups, Jimmy Buffett and the Coral Reefer Band, Boz Scaggs, Max Roach, Ahmad Jamal, the Robert Cray Band, Ry Cooder and David Lindley, Randy Newman, Tito Puente and the Golden Latin Allstars, Horace Silver Brass Ensemble, Aretha Franklin, Wynton Marsalis, Governor Jimmie Davis ("You Are My Sunshine"), Dr. John, the Allman Brothers, Buddy Guy, Stanley Turrentine, Miriam Makeba and Hugh Masekela, George Benson, Shirley Horn Trio, Herbie Hancock Trio (some of these were only at nighttime concerts at other venues throughout the city for which there was an additional admission fee)—plus countless local stars ranging from trad to Zydeco. Needless to say, it was a wide array of talent intended to appeal to a vast and diverse audience.

A NOJ&H press release dated July 23, 1996, stated: "Since its inception in 1970, millions from throughout the United States and all over the world have journeyed to participate in the near-perfect union of the region's unique music, food and culture. Faithful festival-goers view the event as a rite of spring. Nearly 500,000 people attended the 1996 Festival —breaking all previous records. Fueled by picture-perfect weather and stellar performances, the Festival provided a strong jolt to the New Orleans economy, last recorded in 1995 at $200.5 million."

It should be noted that—in addition to the introduction of a new international focus (beginning that year with attention to the music and culture of Haiti)—the seven-day 1996 talent lineup included Phish, Benny Waters, Wynton Marsalis, the Heath Brothers, George Benson, Lionel Hampton, Dee Dee Bridgewater, Indigo Girls, Eddie Palmieri, Dr. John, Buddy Guy, Bela Fleck and the Flecktones, Cassandra Wilson, Van Morrison, Dave Mathews Band, Kenny Barron Trio with Frank Morgan, Lou Donaldson, the Allman Brothers Band, B. B. King, Lloyd Price, Joan Baez (including nighttime performances)—plus numerous local stars representing all genres of local music. Obviously, once again, a program intended to appeal to a wide variety of listeners—but hardly a truly "jazz" festival.

The thirtieth anniversary festival, again a (by-now) standard seven-day affair, took place on April 23–May 2, 1999. In a pre-fest press release, festival producer/director Quint Davis said, "In thirty years, the New Orleans Jazz & Heritage Festival has gone from an instinct to an institution. George Wein's brilliant foresight in designing and producing this Festival in homage to the music and culture of the New Orleans region is confirmed every year during the ten days of Jazz Fest. He knew, and we all know now—thirty years later—that only in New Orleans could such a bold and ambitious celebration flourish."

George Wein, founder and current executive producer of the festival, was honored that year, along with his wife, Joyce, who was considered an "important force" behind the festival from the very beginning.

The press release went on to note the importance of the New Orleans Jazz and Heritage Foundation, Inc., "a 501(c)3 Louisiana nonprofit corporation" whose mission is "to promote, preserve, perpetuate and encourage the music, arts, culture, and heritage indigenous to the New Orleans area." Among the entities supported by the foundation, in addition to the festival itself, are radio station WWOZ, a grants program, the Heritage School of Music providing free music instruction to children, concert series, lecture series, neighborhood street festivals, a "micro-loan program" for small businesses, the LSU Medical Center Musicians' Clinic (as it was then known), a program bringing musicians into the schools, and free and discounted tickets to area residents.

The 1999 lineup included another diverse group of performers: Willie Nelson, Dave Brubeck, George Wein and the Newport Allstars, A Salute to Sinatra with Christopher Riddle (son of Nelson), Santana, Joshua Redman, Jay McShann, Fats Domino, Ray Charles, Dr. John, Poncho Sanchez, Charles Lloyd with Billy Higgins, Cassandra Wilson, Linda Hopkins, New World Funk Ensemble, Los Lobos, Taj Mahal, Branford Marsalis, Widespread Panic, Marcia Ball, Hugh Masekela, Count Basie Orchestra, the Dixie Cups, the Neville Brothers, the Isley Brothers, Hootie and the Blowfish, Third World, Nancy Wilson, Rita Coolidge, Randy Brecker, Harry "Sweets" Edison, Arvell Shaw, Franz Jackson, Cubanismo, Kenny Barron (again including nighttime events), as well as local bands of all styles.

I was fortunate enough to be able to attend most of the festivals during the decade. There have been many high notes, and some not so high. Apart from one or two days of heavy rain, the weather generally cooperated beautifully.

Allison Miner, a close friend of Quint Davis, was a major part of the JazzFest team from its beginnings. In the late '80s, she helped create the annual Music Heritage Stage, at which she would interview some of the prominent artists from each festival. Miner passed away just before Christmas in 1995 at the age of forty-six, and I am fortunate to have attended one of her last JazzFest interviews (Banu Gibson) in that year. The MHS has continued annually since that time with a number of different interviewers. Some of the best I heard thereafter were Michael Gourrier's interview of saxophonists Frank Morgan (1996) and James Moody (1997) and Tom Piazza's conversation with Dr. Billy Taylor in 1998.

It is impossible for me to name which JazzFest performances impressed me most during the decade, but I would have to say that among the best I heard were the Wynton Marsalis Septet (1994); singer Cassandra Wilson, and the Lou Donaldson Quartet with Lonnie Smith (1996); the Herbie Hancock Quartet, and the Bechet tribute performances (1997); singer Carmen Lundy and pianist Danilo Perez (1998); and George Wein's Newport Allstars (Warren Vache, Ken Peplowski, Lew Tabackin, Howard Alden, along with locals Walter Payton and Shannon Powell) and Dave Brubeck (1999). The local bands are often augmented or reconfigured for JazzFest, but they are the same musicians one sees in the clubs or FQF during the year. So, I will not comment upon their JazzFest performances. I have to say, however, that the 1999 performance of Don Vappie's fine Creole Jazz Serenaders was one of my personal highlights for that year's festival.

Matt Goldman of the festival's press office has said that attendance at the fairgrounds was 455,000, making a total 495,000 for the last year of the decade.[12] He goes on to note that that total "was in line with the steady growth of the Fest over the previous years. The 1998 attendance was 447,000, while 2000 was 466,500."

Finally, concluding the decade, a quotation from George Wein addresses the issue of musical (jazz) "purity" at JazzFest: "Let me explain one thing so it is clearly understood. The Lincoln Center Board raises tens or millions of dollars so that Wynton Marsalis can have the freedom to do what he wants to do. In New Orleans, we have to earn the money to give to the Foundation so we can put on the Festival. So nobody is subsidizing the Fest to keep it pure the way some people want it to be pure. Whatever purity we have left—which is a lot, such as the Gospel Tent and the Cajun stage and the archives—is being kept alive by the big name national artists which people resent. It's a simple matter of arithmetic."[13]

COMMEMORATIVE POSTAL CELEBRATIONS

The U.S. Postal Service in New Orleans has a policy of issuing commemorative stamps or "cachets" (commemorative designs on envelopes indicating a special postal or philatelic event) and then hosting celebrations on the days of issue. The practice began in 1991 by honoring **Danny**

Barker and continued on an annual basis throughout the decade. **Louis Armstrong** was the cachet designee in 1994.

Beyond that, the announcement of the Louis Armstrong Stamp by the national postal service was the result of years of politicking and promoting by local groups and individuals. It led to a week-long celebration in the city, from August 28 through September 3, 1995.

The official celebration began on August 31 with a reception and ceremony given by the New Orleans postmaster, Philip Holland, at the Old Mint. A highlight of the event was the unveiling of a plaque honoring Peter Davis, Louis Armstrong's music teacher during the trumpeter's stay in the Colored Waif's Home for Boys (1913–14). The plaque will remain on permanent display in the jazz museum.

The official dedication began on the following day with Wynton Marsalis serving as master of ceremonies before a huge throng at Armstrong Park. Postmaster Holland paid tribute to those whose "tireless efforts" helped to bring the dedication ceremonies to New Orleans, among whom were Bill Farrell of the New Orleans Jazz Club, Don Marquis of the jazz museum, and Eddie Edwards of the (then) Louis Armstrong Foundation (of New Orleans). The unveiling of a replica of the stamp was done by trumpeters Marsalis, Dave Bartholomew (also a former student of Peter Davis), Kermit Ruffins, and Nicholas Payton, along with Houston singer Ruth Brown, who had worked with Armstrong.

Then came the music, with the playing of "What a Wonderful World." A special moment occurred when ninety-year-old trumpeter Doc Cheatham—an adopted New Orleanian—jumped in spontaneously on the last two choruses that, for many, brought Louis to life again. It also brought the crowd to its feet.

Cheatham then took to the podium, saying, "that was the biggest pleasure I ever had in my life." (He later admitted that that had been the first time he'd ever played the song.) He went on to mention his first meeting with Armstrong and how Louis asked him to sit in for him twice at the Vendome Theater in Chicago in the 1920s. "I will never understand that as long as I live," he added with characteristic humility.

The ceremony came to a close when the great trumpeters on hand joined to offer a moving rendition of "Strutting with Some Barbecue." Later, there was a panel discussion on Armstrong and his music chaired by Marsalis. Other panel members were author Tad Jones, Phoebe Jacobs and David Gold of the Armstrong Foundation in New York, writer Stanley Crouch, historian and musician Michael White, and drummer Eddie Edwards, executive of the (now defunct) Armstrong Foundation of New Orleans.

In the evening, the Louisiana Jazz Federation sponsored a musical tribute to Armstrong at the historic Blue Room of the (then) Fairmont Hotel. Trumpeters Cheatham, Bartholomew, and Payton, joined by young New Orleans newcomer Duke Heitger and colleagues provided the music for a crowd of several hundred. There were more concerts later, including a special series at the Palm Court Jazz Café: "Golden Trumpets: Louis Armstrong Week at the Palm Court Café." Cheatham again headed a cast of fine local trumpeters.

The week-long celebration concluded on September 3 with a program of exciting musical performances entitled "The Origins of Jazz in New Orleans," sponsored by the National Park Service and the City of New Orleans at the Mahalia Jackson Theatre in Armstrong Park. As I wrote at the time, "There is much enthusiasm, hope, and planning in the city these days for the development of New Orleans as a center for jazz history, education and performance. Much of what happens, of course, depends on the allocation of funding for the Jazz Park by Congress. Those of us in the area will be keeping our fingers crossed."[14]

What better to symbolize these aspirations than a tribute to Louis Armstrong? Recorded tributes to Satchmo were made by trumpeters Payton and Leroy Jones at the time (and released in the following year): Payton's *Gumbo Nouveau* and Jones's *Props for Pops*. Some fine trumpet playing and top-notch ensemble work, but what is most interesting about them, in my view, is that the trumpeters were putting Louis's music in a contemporary context—and tastefully so, I might add.

Not inappropriately, the next to be recognized by the post office was **Adolphus "Doc" Cheatham**, one of the stars of the Armstrong celebration. Cheatham was honored with an "Official Commemorative Cachet" in a ceremony at the Main Post Office, 701 Loyola Avenue, on Thursday, April 25, 1996. It was just the sixth in that series of cachets and the first non-native to be so honored.

Doc Cheatham was born in Nashville, Tennessee, in June 1905. He developed a liking for New Orleans jazz at an early age, and after moving to Chicago in 1924, he was befriended by two mighty New Orleans jazz pioneers: first, Joe "King" Oliver, who gave him one of his mutes (which Doc used for the rest of his life), and Louis Armstrong (who asked him to sit in for him on two occasions as a young man). Despite his affinity for New Orleans and New Orleans music, it was not until the early 1990s that Doc first visited the city. Once that happened, however, he became an extremely frequent visitor, developing a huge group of friends and admirers here. Indeed, he spent much of the last five years of his life in the city.

On April 25, 1996, he officially became a New Orleanian with the presentation of a key to the city by Mayor Marc Morial at the cachet celebration. Not only did New Orleans totally embrace this gentle and talented man, but he cultivated a liking for the city as well.

As he explained in his autobiography, published in the same year,

> There is one place in the USA where what I've said about the indifference of American audiences [to jazz] is not true. That's New Orleans. In the last few years they've invited me down there several times, and I'm happy to know that the people there are very fond of me. In the last couple of years I've been running down there pretty often, and I've made a couple of albums in New Orleans and played concerts with Butch Thompson as well as appearing on the [Jazz and Heritage] Festival. This is like a new career for me, and I've made friends with many of the musicians there like the drummer Ernie Elly (who I played with in Europe) and the young clarinetist Brian O'Connell, who just gets better all the time and plays on my latest album. So many of the young boys there are getting just a little too modern in their playing. Many, many tourists go there, and they find it disappointing if what they hear is getting too far away from the jazz of the past. Louis Armstrong died too soon, I think that's the reason.[15]

Of course one of the albums that he is referring to is the *Doc Cheatham & Nicholas Payton* Verve CD recorded in New Orleans and released in 1997. The recording was nominated for a 1998 Grammy Award, and the more than eight-minute version of "Stardust" (track #3 on the CD) won that year's Grammy for Best Jazz Instrumental Solo. The observations of respected critic Gary Giddins (1997, 64) say it all: "Cheatham's sound is broader and wobbles a bit in comparison to Payton's tightly focused middle-range attack, but this is no be-kind-to-old-folks date. On 'Star Dust,' Cheatham cuts the little guy to ribbons." The recording was co-produced by his close friend and local manager Andrea DuPlesssis, along with Jerry Brock and George Hocutt. Doc's admiration for the (then) twenty-three-year-old Payton was enormous. "One of the kids who's probably going to be the greatest jazz player of our times is the young trumpet player Nicholas Payton, from New Orleans," he asserts in his book. "He first sat in with me at Sweet Basil [in New York City] when he was just 20 years old, and he's making great strides in his playing. I feel that playing alongside him . . . I'm still learning. In the last year I've played on a couple of concerts at Carnegie Hall alongside Nicholas and Jon Faddis, and George Wein still keeps me busy on his JVC Festival."[16]

Cheatham took very good care of himself as he grew older, though he admitted, "since my 80th birthday I've been waiting around for things to go wrong."[17] Finally, on June 2, 1997, he passed away, less than two weeks before his ninety-second birthday. The music world was deeply saddened and expressed its feelings with emotional tributes in both New York City and New Orleans.

Many of us from New Orleans flew to New York for the wonderful memorial service held for him at Saint Peter's Church in Manhattan on June 8. The crowd was so large that many had to be turned away for fire-safety reasons. Numerous musicians took part in the service, including Wynton Marsalis, Dick Sudhalter, Jon Faddis, Jimmy Owens, Al Grey, Clark Terry, and Cheatham's longtime pianist Chuck Folds. Andrea DuPlessis was the only New Orleanian to speak, and, among many interesting recollections, she noted, "In September [1996] on our way to the studio, the first day of the recording session, he said he probably wouldn't be at his 92nd birthday: 'But that's okay, because I've had a full life. Nobody could ask for more than I have—family, health, career, friends. And I can still play.'"

And, of course, New Orleans also remembered Doc with a memorial tribute and a huge outpouring of love on October 19, 1997, at the Palm Court Café. There were remarks by his family members and many others from the local music community. We should not forget that Doc's whole family, including wife Nellie and trumpet-playing grandson Theo Croker, were considered part of his "New Orleans family" as well.

Music for the event was provided by his *Swinging Down in New Orleans* album's band (on this occasion, without a trumpeter): Butch Thompson, Brian O'Connell, Les Muscutt, Bill Huntington, Peter "Chuck" Badie, and Ernest Elly. Later, in the evening, there was a concert in his honor at Café Brasil with all of the members of the *Doc and Nick* recording band (Lucien Barbarin, Jack Maheu, Thompson, Muscutt, Huntington, and Elly) and Chris Tyle sitting in for Doc. It was the last official tribute to Cheatham in his adopted city, but the memory of him will always be with us.

Much of spring 1997 was devoted to honoring New Orleans jazz pioneer **Sidney Bechet** who, by most accounts, had been born in the Seventh Ward one hundred years earlier. On April 24, 1997, a postal cachet envelope was issued in his memory at a ceremony at La Belle Gallerie on Chartres Street in the French Quarter, where an excellent centennial exhibit had been on display since April 10. (Bechet tributes, in fact, had been taking place in the city since the previous fall.) For a full account of all of the many events that marked the centennial, see my column in *The Mississippi Rag.*[18]

The French Quarter Festival opened that year on April 11. A highlight of opening day was a concert by reedman Jacques Gauthé and his Creole Rice Jazz Band. It chanced that Gauthé's tribute CD, *Echoes of Bechet,* had just been released a few days earlier. Nothing could have been more appropriate. Gauthé (1939–2007), who had been born and raised in a village near Toulouse, France, met Bechet in 1952—a year after the latter moved to France for good. He had been inspired by Bechet and his protégé Claude Luter (1923–2006) to study the clarinet. In 1957, Bechet and Luter played a concert in Toulouse and the latter invited Gauthé to sit in with them. While he remembers being "scared to death," it all seems to have gone well enough. In any case, Gauthé stayed in touch with Bechet until his death in France in 1959. Thereafter Luter became something of a mentor to him. Jacques and his wife, Nellie, moved to New Orleans in 1968, and the Crescent City remained his base until he died after playing a concert in France in June 2007. Gauthé was a fine soprano saxophonist and clarinetist in the Bechet style. He was utterly devoted to the music of Bechet, but, in my opinion, he never received the recognition he deserved in his hometown in the United States.[19]

There were more performances honoring Bechet at JazzFest 1997, which concluded in the first week of May. Claude Luter was in town, and he and Dr. Michael White honored the legend with a performance on May 3—before Luter joined Gauthé later in the day with more of the same. Then came more Bechet music with French reedman Fabrice Zammarchi and Canadian saxophonist Jim Galloway. Finally, Bob Wilber, who had been tutored by and lived with Bechet as a teenager in New York, came from England to bring that day's music to a close.

Beyond the musical tributes to Bechet, there was a Bechet Centennial Conference that opened on May 5. The opening reception included as honored guests the French ambassador to the United States, the French consul general in New Orleans, Mayor Morial and members of the Bechet family—most notably his son Daniel Sidney Bechet, a personable young man. Daniel is also a musician, leading two bands in his homeland. There was more music by Gauthé and Luter. The conference itself began on May 6 and included a number of distinguished participants: John Chilton, the British author of an excellent Bechet biography; Fabrice Zammarchi (also the author of a handsome biography of Buddy DeFranco), who discussed the last ten years of Bechet's life in France; Wolfram Knauer, German jazz scholar; Bob Wilber, who called Bechet "a born teacher"; and a panel that included local musicians and jazz educators Alvin Batiste, Harold Battiste, Kidd Jordan, and Ellis Marsalis.

The conference was brought to a close with a brass-band parade—said to be the largest of its kind—from Jackson Square to Congo Square via St. Peter Street. The intent was to dedicate the bronze bust of Bechet, which is displayed in Congo Square in Armstrong Park. It is a replica of the famous original set up by the French in Juan-les-Pins, France, in 1960, the year following his death.

A final USPS philatelic celebration held in the city during the decade was the official unveiling of four new commemorative stamps to four of the greatest female gospel singers. Needless to say, New Orleans's own **Mahalia Jackson** (1911–1972), considered by most the greatest of them all, made the city an especially appropriate locale for the ceremony. Jackson got her start here, at Mount Moriah Baptist Church, before moving to Chicago in 1927. She made her first recording in 1937 and, by the 1950s, she was touring the world and being received by royalty and heads of state. She was honored at the ceremony by Joshua Nelson, who sang "Move On Up a Little Higher." The program's master of ceremonies, Kirk Franklin, praised Nelson for making a career of recreating Jackson's style.

This event took place on July 15, 1998, and it was held in the (then called) Louisiana Superdome, where thousands gathered as part of the Full Gospel Baptist Church Fellowship's 1998 Conference. The other singers honored with stamps were Sister Rosetta Tharpe, Roberta Martin, and Clara Ward. All were recognized with songs sung by national gospel performers. Indeed, the occasion turned out to be a real gospel fest with some of the industry's biggest stars. The rousing finale consisted of all featured singers plus a huge massed choir of hundreds of voices. The thousands in attendance, who had been on their feet throughout most of the program, were totally into it by that moment.

I have been exposed to a great deal of good gospel singing since moving to this city, but I had never experienced—and doubtless never will again—the thrill of this event. It was extremely impressive. And I had the good fortune of witnessing it from the foot of the stage itself![20]

MEMBERS OF THE LOCAL MUSIC COMMUNITY WHO MADE A DIFFERENCE IN THE 1990S

There are so many local residents who, though mostly not musicians, did so much and gave so much of themselves in support of the local jazz scene that it is impossible to acknowledge all of them by name. I am thinking here of the likes of Dick Allen, Helen Arlt, Dr. Connie Atkinson, Jerry Brock, Mina Crais, Julie Fishelson, Mike Gourrier, Sue Hall, Fred Hatfield, George Hocutt, Gene Hyden, Don "Moose" Jamison, Elaine Jones, Helen and Ralph Judy, Dr. Al Kennedy, Don Marquis, Dr. Kurt and Sue Nicewander, Jon Pult, Mary and Ron Saltarrelli, Dodie Simmons, Willie Spoden and Ann Parker, and John Titsworth—and the list could go on and on. Then there is Nina Buck of the Palm Court Café who, despite hiring the musicians and providing the facilities for their performances, has gone way beyond her official duties in support of individual musicians and the music in general.

But there is one person who did so much, always without fanfare, and stands out in that respect. That would be **Andrea DuPlessis**. Andrea was born in Wisconsin and moved with her parents at a young age to New Orleans in 1949.[21] Her mother was a jazz lover, so she was exposed to a great deal of New Orleans jazz at an early age. She says that she started to take the music seriously when she went off to college in Oklahoma. "We didn't hear very much of it there," she recalls. "I was really fond of Percy and Willie Humphrey's band. Every chance I got, when I came home from school, I would go to Preservation Hall. That was in the early '60s."[22]

So, that was the beginning of her devotion and commitment to jazz. Her involvement became more direct in 1991, when she produced a CD featuring two New Orleans clarinetists, veteran Willie Humphrey and young Brian O'Connell. It was called *Two Clarinets on the Porch,* a clear allusion to the large porch of the DuPlessis residence at the corner of Bourbon and Esplanade in the French Quarter. That porch was the site of annual Mardi Gras parties put on by Andrea and her husband Dr. Gorst DuPlessis, and all came to feature live music. But that was before the record was produced.

"I had just met Brian O'Connell," she explains (in response to a question about how the music got started),

> and found out that he had come from Minnesota to study with Willie Humphrey, to learn from Willie. I'd never hired a band before in my life, so I asked him if he would put together some people and what it

> would cost. He said he thought he might be able to get Willie Humphrey, and I believe he wrote a grant requesting enough pay for Willie. So, the party became Willie's lesson to Brian. Willie would do all kinds of fun things that would make Brian learn new things on the clarinet. Sometimes you'd hear Willie say, "You can do it. Go ahead, you can do it." So, that's the way it was every year. Willie played every year, except for one when he had to tour with the Hall, until he passed away [June 1994]. Whatever band we have—Brian's the leader, he's traditionally the leader—it's spontaneous and fun. It's never routine.

Those Mardi Gras parties have become legendary in the city's music community. They always take place on the Saturday before Fat Tuesday. Given the success of the first, it was not long before she and Brian were thinking about doing another record.

> Brian had said that he would really love to play with Doc Cheatham. I had heard Cheatham a few months before that at JazzFest. Then Dick Allen encouraged me to go to a concert at the Palm Court to hear him again. When I heard Doc Cheatham play, it was magical to me. The sound was just beautiful. It was '93, maybe. I didn't even speak to him that night. I just left, but I thought he was fabulous. The year before that he played JazzFest with Wynton Marsalis. That was his first year down here. It think that was '92.
>
> So, when Brian said he would like to do a record with Doc Cheatham, I wondered if he would even ever come back to New Orleans and how we would find this person. We went over to Sue Hall's house, and she got him on the phone and introduced us on the phone. I asked him if he would consider recording with us down in New Orleans, and he said, "Why, certainly." I was so amazed. He came down that JazzFest month, and we recorded [in 1994].

The album was called *Swinging Down in New Orleans*. It was released in the same year.

Doc loved the record, so he and Andrea remained in close touch thereafter. "He liked the link to New Orleans," she says.

> One time somebody asked him if he had any regrets in life and he said, "One, that I wasn't born in New Orleans." He explained that meant, if he had grown up around the sound of New Orleans musicians, he would have learned the style like he wanted to learn it. That's not to say that he wasn't happy to have come from Nashville. One day he called up and just said, "I think you should be my New Orleans manager. It's easier that way." He didn't want complications in this time in his life. If something were simplified, if he could get a phone call, come down, play the job, enjoy the people, eat the food, have fun, be paid, and go home, it was a lot nicer for him than having to deal with contracts and arrangements and plane tickets. I did all that for him, and he loved it. He loved coming to New Orleans. He loved catfish for breakfast, and grits and many things which he shouldn't have eaten.

There were thoughts about a second volume of the *Swinging Down in New Orleans* CD, and he and Nicholas Payton went into the studio to record some things for it in August 1994. The recording has yet to be released, but, according to DuPlessis, it will appear as *Swinging Down in New Orleans, Volume 2.*

The two were back together in the studio in September 1996, however. The result, of course, was the Grammy-winning *Doc Cheatham & Nicholas Payton,* which appeared in the following year on the Verve label. Andrea was joined by Jerry Brock and George Hocutt as co-producers. Hocutt estimated that it would sell 25,000 copies, though it probably would show a profit with 10–15,000. It eventually sold nearly 30,000.[23]

Doc Cheatham played opening day of JazzFest, April 25, 1997. There was a huge crowd, and he played well. Then, near the end of his set, he announced, "I have a surprise for you. I'm so happy to bring out my partner—you may know him—Nicholas Payton. They played two tunes ("Jada" and "Jeepers Creepers"), and the crowd went berserk. Doc died less than two months later.

"For me," Andrea (who has endless Cheatham stories) reflected,

> the main thing was that Doc came to New Orleans, something that he wanted to do all his life. To him, it was a very significant part of

> his life. He loved coming down for the Louie Armstrong stamp issue event. He was a big star at that. He loved it. And because of that the Post Office did a cachet of him the next year. So, one thing led to another. When Doc passed away, I decided I would never manage anyone again. I figured I would do something in education. Just before the Grammy event, [bassist] Bill Huntington invited me to come hear him perform in a duet with [pianist] Henry Butler at the Sheraton. I enjoyed it very much. I enjoyed hearing Henry again—I had heard him twice before—and meeting him. He talked about his interest in education of blind and visually impaired children.

To make a long story rather shorter, DuPlessis and Butler developed a relationship akin to that which she had with Doc Cheatham. She helped Butler identify and arrange for educational sessions between him and visually impaired children all over the country. "Some of the things that have helped me with Henry's projects were begun when I was working with Doc," she says. "Many of the good things that have come about with Henry's projects are extensions of relationships with people I knew when I worked with Doc. Another person I am working with now, Wade Barnes, was introduced to me by Doc at Sweet Basil in New York. Wade is also a gifted musician who is dedicated to a career as a professional musician, and he also has degrees in history, education, and music, which enable him to communicate educationally and musically with students from Pre-K through post-graduate years."

Andrea's approach to working with Henry Butler was different from that with Doc Cheatham. Butler was at a much earlier stage of his career than Cheatham, who was near the end of his. "Henry is a brilliant intellect," she says.

> He had such a variety of skills and talent that he's pulled in many different directions just by invitation. He has less time to communicate with people on a day-to-day basis. He has to be careful to remember to make a living because there's a side of Henry that would like to spend a lot of time with the kids and education. But he has to pay the bills. He has to put that first.

> We decided, wherever Henry performed, if it were possible to reach children in other cities, we would do our best to make that happen. Last year [1998] Henry performed in Tucson, AZ, and we went to the school for the blind there. We've only been on this for a year, maybe a year and a half. We also went to the California School for the Blind in Fremont. He had done this in camps several years before, but he hadn't done this on gigs recently because there wasn't anyone probably to work with him in the way I do. Most people want to be paid, most people don't have the time, and he doesn't have the time to do it himself. He needs help getting it done, my expenses are paid for, I'll do it. Or I'll set it up and not be there if it works out for that to happen.

A very interesting example of that was the time he was playing a blues gig at a barbecue place in Austin, where the Texas School for the Blind is located. Andrea engineered a session where Butler would play a free concert for the whole school. The school authorities did not know her, nor did they know Henry. There was some resistance because, as she put it, people don't believe somebody is doing something for nothing. Nevertheless, it was there that they encountered an extraordinary talent, a young pianist by the name of T. J. Wade. Butler took him on as a special project because of his unusual musical potential, and he became the first youngster to be part of the Henry Butler Institute of Summer Studies in New Orleans. He made a profound impression on the various audiences for whom he performed in our city.

On another occasion, Butler was playing at the Green Mill in Chicago, and Andrea arranged for two free workshops there. When asked how they identified these venues, she says with a laugh, "That's my job, and it's not all that easy. It's hard to find them. In this case, the Green Mill guy told me about it."

So, as the decade (and century) came to a close, Andrea DuPlessis was deeply involved in the types of projects described above. Beyond that, she was initiating another relationship with a New York drummer by the name of Wade Barnes whom she had met through Doc Cheatham. As she put it,

> I'm loyal to Henry's projects because I believe in his motivation and what he's doing, and I think he's making a difference in many ways. To have crossed paths with Henry Butler enriches the lives of many people.
>
> I feel the same with the project I'm doing with Wade Barnes. He is an individual who has been a teacher for 20 years—a special ed teacher, among other things—in the New York Public School System. Wade has spent a lot of time in schools telling the children about the history of jazz. He is a very dedicated person who cares about the kids and his students. One of his interests is to make people aware of people he considers his mentors. Right now he is telling the story of [reedman] Cecil Payne and [bassist] Leonard Gaskin and that generation of player. And he performs with them. He had asked me to help him tell their story by putting them on a recording. So, even though I don't have a background in bebop, the idea interests me. The recording will be on the Progressive label and will be out in September [1999].[24]

So, that is, in short, how Andrea DuPlessis spent her decade musically. If there is one common thread in these stories, it would be her dedication to jazz and to children and helping similarly dedicated musicians provide the link between the two.[25]

JAZZ EDUCATION IN THE 1990S

The **Heritage School of Music**, sponsored by the New Orleans Jazz and Heritage Foundation, was started by Edward "Kidd" Jordan in 1990. It provides free, weekly after-school instruction to teenagers from the whole of the New Orleans region and aims to provide the basics of music performance and theory. Jordan, who is assisted by a talented faculty of local jazz musicians, says, "I try to help them with their instrument and with the jazz vocabulary. Then they can take it and do something with it." A tough taskmaster, he stresses music fundamentals in his teaching. Though admired by his students, he says, "I'm not looking for people to like me." Alumni include trumpeter-trombonist Troy "Trombone Shorty" Andrews and trumpeter Shamarr Allen. A number of the students have also gone on to attend major music conservatories in the country.

The Heritage School was headquartered at Southern University, New Orleans (SUNO) for many years. After the Katrina disaster (2005), it moved to Lusher Charter High School, expanding in 2007 to include Saturday classes at Dillard University and other local schools. (In May of 2013, the NOJ&H Foundation announced that its new home will be in the renovated building at 1225 North Rampart named in honor of George and Joyce Wein.)

Another new program for young people was initiated in mid-decade. The **Louis "Satchmo" Armstrong Summer Jazz Camp** was founded in 1995 with the support of the City of New Orleans. Mayor Morial called it "the first government-produced jazz education program in the city's history." Later, however, private, non-profit funding replaced that from city government.

Initially, the camp was a one-week affair with some thirty-five students. It has since grown to a three-week curriculum training three times that number, with an age range of ten to twenty-one. Students have come from far and wide, not just from New Orleans. The program has again been directed by Kidd Jordan, assisted by a host of top-notch local musicians. Instruction is in brass, woodwinds, piano, acoustic and electric bass, drums, percussion, guitar, and music composition; swing dance and vocal music are also offered. Early on, the camp was hosted by the University of New Orleans. It has since moved to Loyola University.

Apart from the above, the situation as described in Chapter 3 pretty much continued into the decade of the '90s. Clyde Kerr Jr. headed a very successful jazz program at NOCCA. Most of the local "young lions" cited below were NOCCA graduates. Irvin Mayfield speaks admiringly of Kerr and his years there. "Clyde Kerr totally changed my life," he has said.[26]

Likewise, Ellis Marsalis was now fully installed at UNO. His reputation drew talented students from all over the country. Many stayed around to graduate. Others—like Mayfield—remained for shorter periods, but went on to succeed in the business nevertheless.

John Mahoney remained in charge of the jazz studies program at Loyola University. He also led the Loyola University Jazz Band, which was recognized for Outstanding Performance at the Elmhurst College Jazz Festival in 1994 to add to its earlier reputation.

The Loyola Jazz Ensemble Festival, an annual multiday program to evaluate and help train young jazz bands, began in the late 1960s. Under the supervision of Mahoney, it regularly featured notable guest artists and clinicians. The lineup of guest clinicians in the 1990s was particularly impressive: Phil Woods (1990), Clark Terry (1991), John Fedchock (1992), Hal Galper Trio (1993), Benny Golson (1994), Lew Soloff (1995), Bill Watrous (1996), Ed Thigpen (1997), Bob Shepherd (1998), and Marvin Stamm (1999).

Finally, apart from (drummer) John Joyce's history-of-jazz course in the Music Department, there was no formal jazz education at Tulane University until 1995. At that time, an M.A. in musicology with a special concentration in New Orleans jazz was introduced, but it did not begin to flourish until the following decade.

YOUNG LIONS AND SOME OF THE TOP BANDS OF THE DECADE

A large number of veteran musicians in the city—many of whom are local jazz legends—passed away during the 1990s. Fortunately, an at least equally large number of unusually talented musicians came of age during the same decade. Generally speaking, those would be the young people born in the 1970s. Hence, these gifted youngsters began to hit the scene as teenagers or in their early twenties in the '90s. Some were homegrown while others moved to the city from elsewhere. It would be impossible for me to name all of these young musicians, but I will make note of those who made a particularly favorable impression on me.

The locals would include (with birth years): trumpeter Mark Braud (1973), trumpeter Leon "Kid Chocolate" Brown (1978), clarinetist-saxophonist Ryan Burrage (1974), trumpeter Mark Chatters (1971), drummer

Gerald French (1970), bassist Roland Guerin (1969), trombonist Corey Henry (1975), bassist Ben Jaffe (1971), trombonist Ronnell "Roo" Johnson (1976), trumpeter Marlon Jordan (1970), bassist Kerry Lewis (1973), percussionist Jason Marsalis (1977), trumpeter Irvin Mayfield (1977), trumpeter Nicholas Payton (1973), drummer Adonis Rose (1975), and trombonist Stephen Walker (1979). Despite his even more tender age, trombonist/trumpeter Troy "Trombone Shorty" Andrews (1986) was already a well-known name around town by the mid-'90s.

Others from the neighborhood were drummer Brian Blade (1970) and bassist Mitchell Player (1970), from Shreveport; the Brackman brothers, cornetist Chuck (1972) and clarinetist Bruce (1975), from Baton Rouge.

Several of these young men achieved national reputations before the end of the decade. Probably the quickest to be widely recognized were trumpeters Marlon Jordan and Nicholas Payton. Jordan made three albums for the Columbia label between 1988 and 1992, his first (*For You Only*) being named "one of the best debut albums of the year" by the *Washington Post.* Payton made four albums for Verve between 1994 and 1997, the last his acclaimed collaboration with Doc Cheatham (*Doc Cheatham & Nicholas Payton*) that garnered a Grammy award.

One young female singer (among several) made a particularly favorable impression on me during the 1990s. Christina Machado (ca. 1973), a New Orleanian of Cuban parents, first appeared on the local club scene (after graduating from American University in Washington, D.C.) in the last half of the decade. I first heard her at Storyville District, though she performed at Snug Harbor, Meridien, and numerous other venues (including a series devoted to Ellington and Strayhorn with Peter Martin on piano at the city's newest cabaret, Le Chat Noir).

Machado's voice was mature for her age and her delivery warm—indeed, sultry—and tasteful. She always seemed to perform with first-rate musicians. That is no more evident than on her debut album, which appeared in 2000. Titled *Gone with the Wind,* it features a nice selection of jazz standards, revealing her talent as a singer of ballads as well as swingers. (One tune, "Free Yourself," is an original composition by her and her good friend Nicholas Payton.) Her colleagues on the recording included Payton (on trumpet, flugelhorn, and trombone); saxophonists Brice

Winston and John Ellis; pianists Peter Martin and Michael Esneault; Roland Guerin, bass; Adonis Rose, drums; and Kenyatta Simon, percussion. I looked for big things in the future from Ms. Machado, but that was not to be since she disappeared inexplicably from the local scene early in the next decade.

Among those from out of town were bassist Neil Caine (1973); trumpeter Jeremy Davenport (1971), pianist Peter Martin (1971), and bassist David Pulphus (1973), all from St. Louis (there has been a long and close musical relationship between these two river towns); clarinetist (and saxophonist) Evan Christopher (1969) and bassist Matt Perrine (1970), from California; trumpeter Duke Heitger (1968), from Ohio; trombonist Mike Owen (1970), from the United Kingdom; and pianist Frederick Sanders (1971), from Dallas. While some of the newcomers came with a primary interest in modern jazz, others—like their predecessors from previous decades—were only interested in traditional jazz. Christopher, Davenport, and Heitger probably made the biggest splashes upon their arrival in town, soon gaining national attention.

Heitger (Christopher was a fill-in from time to time) became a key member of one of the top bands in the city, **Banu Gibson and the New Orleans Hot Jazz**. The group had already become a popular touring band in the previous decade. Gibson's failure to solidify a permanent base in the city meant that much of the band's work continued to come on the road—at festivals, clubs, and concerts. The latter now included appearances with the likes of the St. Louis Symphony Orchestra, the Boston Pops Orchestra, and the Hollywood Bowl Orchestra. The out-of-town press repeatedly referred to the band's great charts and its outstanding musicians. By mid-decade the lineup looked pretty much like this: Heitger, trumpet; Tom Fischer, clarinet and saxophones; David Sager, trombone; David Boeddinghaus, piano and musical director; Kerry Lewis, bass; Jeff Hamilton, drums; and Gibson, tenor guitar, banjo and vocals—a truly all-star cast.

The musical style of the group had changed (or expanded) by this time. Originally, the band had been heavily into the music of the '20s (with instrumentation that included tuba and banjo). But now the swing sound (with string bass and guitar) became more in evidence. As Boeddinghaus has said, "Not one of us is from New Orleans and, more importantly, we never really have been trying to promote ourselves as a New Orleans–type jazz group. New Orleans is one of the few cities in the United States of America where a group of people wanting to play one of the many different types of earlier styles of jazz can do so." He goes on to amplify, "It so happens that, at this point in time, we perform in a manner comparable and similar to a band from the mid-'30s. I could fudge on that on either end. We have enough understanding and love of earlier jazz that, if we want to play a jazz composition of the late '20s, we'll sound like it. We switch gears a little bit. There is such a vast amount of jazz recorded in the '20s and '30s by so many different artists, and yet they all improvised within that same melodic and harmonic framework."[27] This particular group of musicians was, in my opinion, the best that Gibson has ever put together.

Something of the same may be said about another local band with, in some respects, a similar profile. With the hiring of drummer Richard "Dickie" Taylor in 1990, the (new) **Dukes of Dixieland** reached a high point in quality and stability. (Taylor [1940–2010] had once been a member of Banu Gibson's band.) The Dukes started the decade with J. B. Scott in the trumpet chair, but he was soon replaced by Kevin Clark (now the leader of the Dukes). The fine clarinetist Tim Laughlin was with the band for most of the decade, as was the excellent pianist/composer/arranger Tom McDermott. Trombonist Al Barthlow (1932–2010), like Scott, could be heard on the band's first two recordings of the decade; but he was replaced by Ben Smith, who remained with the band until his retirement in the present century. The bassist for most of the decade (and following) was Everett Link.

Taylor's experience and maturity gave a stability and new life to the young band. They recorded six albums during the decade, ranging from traditional Dukes material to tributes to Jelly Roll, the Bob Cats, and Bix, culminating with a Grammy-nominated gospel-tinged CD called simply "Gloryland." Like Banu's band, the Dukes presented an ensemble of talented musicians. They differed in a couple of notable respects, however: the Dukes had a permanent base at home, the riverboat *Natchez*, where they played nightly; and they unashamedly aimed to reach a wider audience. Boeddinghaus would surely not allow Banu's organization to attempt some of the things that the Dukes have done.

Taylor first saw the original Dukes of Dixieland in 1954, in Lombard, Illinois, near his home in Chicago. "I want to play," he told me, "like the Dukes play because I remember the original Dukes. I want the band to sound like the [original] Dukes. I want the same enthusiasm. I like the little shtick on the stage because it makes the music sellable. For me, the Dukes' sound was free-wheeling New Orleans stuff. They were all good players, but they had a tremendously wonderful time playing the music. The more traditional sounds—like Chris Tyle and his group, Preservation Hall, Eddie Bayard's band—they're great, but I want to have the open style, the dixieland style. Stuff like Santo Pecora and Murphy Campo and those guys. I like that."[28] In addition to its steady gig on the *Natchez,* the band made numerous appearances in concert and at festivals throughout the country. These Dukes were undoubtedly the classic contemporary example of the "Dixieland" style.[29]

Turning to more contemporary sounds, probably the hottest new band in town by the end of the decade was the exciting **Los Hombres Calientes**. First conceived by trumpeter Irvin Mayfield, then just twenty, and percussionist Bill Summers about 1997, the band made its debut at Snug Harbor in February 1998 and shortly thereafter released its first CD, *Los Hombres Calientes* (which also happened to be Mayfield's recording debut). That recording was a smash hit instantly, becoming the number-one-selling CD at the 1998 New Orleans Jazz and Heritage Festival. It repeated that honor in the following year, when it won the *Billboard* Latin Jazz Album of the Year. The core band on that recording was Mayfield, trumpet; Summers, percussion and vocals; Jason Marsalis, drums; David Pulphus, bass; Victor "Red" Atkins, piano; and Yvette Bostic-Summers, percussion, vocals—plus other guest vocalists. With that CD, the band was off and running.

Referring to Herbie Hancock's *Headhunters* album, Mayfield says,

> The album was Bill Summers' first recording session and it's how I first learned of him. To know Bill Summers is to know his passion for the drum and history of everything connected to it. When I was

> twenty and Bill was fifty, we created a band called Los Hombres Calientes. Our mission was to show the musical and cultural connections between New Orleans and Haiti, Cuba, Brazil, Trinidad, Jamaica, and other port cities. It was a quest for the uniquely vibrant cultures that may be hidden from our ears. We eventually recorded most of our records in these port cities. Over the next ten years, we faced every challenge and argument that could arise between co-band leaders with a thirty-year age difference. It was our differences, however, that made for some really diversified and energetic music.[30]

The band released two more CDs in each of following years.

New Orleans's close ties, musically and otherwise, with the cultures of the Caribbean and Latin America are a well-known historical fact. This recording, along with a national trend, may have played a significant role in stimulating a renewed interest locally in the musical connections between New Orleans and the Latin world that would manifest itself more fully in the following decades with the work of local musicians such as saxophonist Ray Moore, pianist/composer Tom McDermott, and trombonist Rick Trolsen.

Another band in the broadly "traditional" vein that appeared in the last half of the decade was the **Creole Jazz Serenaders** (CJS), led by multi-instrumentalist Don Vappie.[31] It is a tight eight-piece unit that plays a diverse program of traditional tunes, many of which are less than well known, associated with important bands of the past—along with a variety of numbers, often of Caribbean origin, sung by Vappie in French. All tunes are transcribed for the band's instrumentation by Vappie himself. The group's style would be considered broadly in the repertory genre, but, since it always includes outstanding soloists, there is no attempt to slavishly imitate the original works.

The CJS was born in 1995 and made its first public appearance at JazzFest in the following year. Their debut CD, *Creole Blues*, was released in 1997 and received very favorable attention. Their second release, *In Search of King Oliver*, appeared in 1998. The personnel diverged slightly from that of the first recording, and most played historic instruments.

A particularly memorable series of performances by the band took place in the spring of 1998. I attended the last of the three concerts, at Le Petit Theatre in the French Quarter on May 1. The series was a tribute to Jelly Roll Morton and the little-known music of his last years. It was billed as "Jelly Roll's Big New Band." The original scores were discovered in the Bill Russell archive in the Historical New Orleans Collection. The concert concluded with a fourteen-piece band playing four of Morton's tunes, the most fascinating of which (in my view) was called "Ganjam." It was quite unlike anything I'd ever heard by Morton, reminding me of the so-called jungle style of early Ellington. This deserves to be more widely heard. Vappie told me that all three nights were recorded, so there would be a possibility for an eventual CD. To my knowledge, no such recording has yet appeared.

A member of CJS's debut recording was saxophonist-clarinetist-composer **Victor Goines** (1961), a New Orleans native (and a personal favorite). A graduate of Loyola University, he later did graduate work with Ellis Marsalis at Virginia Commonwealth University. His debut recording as a leader was *Genesis* on the AFO label (1992), which also included some of the "lions" mentioned above: Payton, Martin, and Blade. In the following year he became associated with Wynton Marsalis and Jazz at Lincoln Center and made numerous recordings in that context. Apart from his considerable talents as an instrumentalist, Goines has achieved a national reputation as a jazz educator. Among his several academic appointments were director of the jazz program at Juilliard School and, as of this writing, professor of music and director of jazz studies at Northwestern University in Evanston, Illinois.

Finally, this might serve as a reminder of what seemed to me to be a revival of big-band music in the city. Perhaps the phenomenon was due to the popularity of "swing dancing" at the time. In any case, several new ensembles made their debuts in the '90s.

The Contemporary Arts Center (CAC) on Camp Street, under then-director Jay Weigel, featured an ad hoc big band for several performances during the decade. In January 1993, for example, a wonderful sixteen-piece aggregation was assembled to perform the big-band music of Thad Jones. The group included Tony Dagradi, Fred Kemp, Cindy Mayes, Ray Moore, and Michael Pierce, saxophones; Chuck Easterling, Jamil Sharif,

Clyde Kerr Jr., and Nicholas Payton, trumpets; Richard Erb, John Mahoney, Rick Trolsen, and John Touchy, trombones; David Torkanowsky, piano; James Singleton, bass, and Johnny Vidacovich, drums—an all-star cast, clearly.

Torkanowsky was back to put together another band for a series of three concerts in 1996 called "Celebration of the Voice," featuring local singers George French, Johnny Adams (1932–1998), and Germaine Bazzle. He emphasized the "little-known but substantial big band legacy" in the city. The concerts were recorded, and the album, *Mood Indigo*, appeared on the Rounder label in 1997.

The impressive feature of this album, in my opinion, is the outstanding makeup of the band selected by Torkanowsky. The sidemen included Jeremy Davenport, Eric Jakebson, Nicholas Payton, and Willie Singleton, trumpets; Mark Mullins, Rick Trolsen, John Touchy, and Brian O'Neill, trombones; Tony Dagradi, Ed Petersen, Wess "Warm Daddy" Anderson, Ray Moore, and Victor Goines, reeds; Peter Martin, piano; Christopher Thomas, bass; and Herlin Riley, drums. The arrangements left plenty of space for solos, and conductor Torkanowsky, following in the footsteps of his father (one-time music conductor of the New Orleans Symphony Orchestra), gave them a very tight presentation.

The **CAC Jazz Orchestra**, as it came to be called, performed, with varying personnel, on many subsequent occasions. They did, for example, a memorable two-night concert series in the following year under the direction of saxophonist Tony Dagradi. It was called "Satchmo at the CAC: A Louis Armstrong Big Band Tribute" and featured trumpeters Charlie Miller (a longtime musical director for Dr. John and sometimes overlooked in the jazz community), Wendell Brunious, and Jamil Sharif.

For me, these CAC concerts were a highlight of the decade. Weigel, who is no longer at the CAC, deserves much credit for re-igniting interest in the big bands locally. The participating musicians were always of the highest quality.

Then there was the **Crescent City Big Band**, led by drummer Brian Preen, which came into existence in 1993. Their self-titled debut CD appeared in 1999. The band could be heard periodically at Tipitina's and the Treasure Chest Casino. The **Northshore Jazz Orchestra**, led by saxophonist Mike Wagner, made its debut in public in the fall of 1998. It seems to have disappeared shortly thereafter.

Trumpeter Chuck Easterling led a fine band—**Chuck Easterling's Swingafonic Orchestra**—in the '80s and early '90s. Their public appearances, however, were sporadic (at Snug Harbor periodically, JazzFest, and the French Quarter Festival). Saxophonist Ray Moore recalls: "It was a good band. At times, at the beginning, we read Basie charts. Later, it became more of a repertory band. I don't know if you heard us when we were doing the old '30s stuff, or some of late stuff too. In the early days, we played late nights at the Absinthe Bar on Bourbon Street, and we'd play from like two to five a.m. Guys would get off their gigs. . . . We'd get off our gig at the Blue Room at 12:30—there were several of us—and we'd find our way to the Absinthe. I remember the sun coming up more than once after one of those rehearsals."

Moore then goes on, "Lots of good guys would come through that band. That's where I met Rick Trolsen, as I recall. Paul McGinley played in that band off and on—different guys that would come through town. Some stayed, some left. But it was a good band."[32]

In 1992, saxophonist Al Belletto took over that band, retaining many of the band's sidemen. It became the **Al Belletto Big Jazz Band**. They, too, played the local festivals and appeared regularly for a time at the Red Room on St. Charles Avenue. (This was a great venue for dining and dancing. It's a pity that it didn't remain in business longer.) The band recorded a fine CD, *Jazznocracy*, on the (local) Red Hot label in 1997. The sixteen-piece outfit's personnel included some of best in town, many of whom also worked with other local big bands (for example, the CAC Orchestra): trumpeters Bobby Campo, Jamil Sharif, trombonist Rick Trolsen (whom Belletto called "the best trombone player in the country"), pianist/trombonist/composer/arranger/educator John Mahoney, saxophonist Ray Moore, bassist Ed Wise, and drummer Johnny Vidacovich (about whom Belletto says, "I had never played with anybody that musical"). It's difficult to keep a big band together without steady gigs, and, given their many other commitments, it was impossible for Belletto (or any of the other leaders mentioned here) to keep this talented group together on a regular basis.

The **John Mahoney Big Band** was also first assembled in 1992 by trombonist, pianist, composer, and arranger John Mahoney. It's strictly a concert band (fifteen to twenty pieces) and performs many of the leader's compositions and arrangements. Mahoney is careful to get the best local musicians for the aggregation, hence explaining why a number of the band members are also heard with some of the above ensembles. "Essential men to get," he says, "are Ray Moore on lead alto, Bobby Campo on lead trumpet, B. J. McGibney on bass trombone, along with competent rhythm section players. My son, David, has held the drum chair for several years. I almost always have Bryan Graber for solos on trumpet, and, more recently, Dave Blask. Clarence Johnson [III] is a blast in the first tenor chair, whenever I can get him. But every chair is important!"[33] The Mahoney band has appeared frequently at Snug Harbor as well as the local festivals and numerous special events in the city.

Finally, while slightly off base, I would note the number of top-flight New Orleans musicians who have toured with **Harry Connick Jr. and His Big Band**, founded in 1990. The band has included Shannon Powell on drums (since 1998); bassist Neal Caine (though originally from St. Louis); trumpeters Jeremy Davenport (another St. Louis native) and Mark Braud; clarinetist Louis Ford; and trombonists Mark Mullins, Craig Klein, and Lucien Barbarin (also vocals). It is remarkable how Connick can manage to juggle so successfully the variety of artistic endeavors in which he is involved.

THE BRASS BAND SCENE IN THE '90S

Veteran brass-band trumpeter Milton Batiste, who had been playing with the popular Olympia Brass Band for thirty years, could say in 1995 that there were then more brass bands than ever in the city. That is probably true, but there would be many more before too long.

The "explosion" that we referred to in the last chapter continued into the decade under consideration. Traditional bands such as Algiers

(Ruddley Thibodeaux), Olympia (Milton Batiste and Harold "Duke" Dejan), Onward (Placide Adams), Doc Paulin's (Ernest "Doc" Paulin), and Treme (Benny Jones and Lionel Batiste) continued to play an important role, especially in second-line parades and the so-called "jazz funerals."[34]

While some new bands (such as the Young Olympians, led by trumpeter Mervin "Kid Merv" Campbell), were spinoffs of the established traditional bands, most were in the more recent tradition begun by the Hurricane and the Dirty Dozen. The Dozen was still popular (especially in Europe), but the consistent winner in *OffBeat* magazine's annual "Best of the Beat" brass-band category was the Rebirth Brass Band—despite cofounder Kermit Ruffins's departure in 1993. *OffBeat* began to track what they initially termed "contemporary" brass bands in 1995, and Rebirth won each year (with the exception of 1996, when Treme won) through 2000 (and, in fact, well beyond that).

Once the fascination with the neo–brass bands became widespread, a host of new bands appeared on the scene. They often consisted, in large part, of young, relatively inexperienced musicians. Irvin Mayfield, even as a teenager himself, represented the point of view of many more senior musicians locally when he spoke (in 1996) about the inexperience of some of these young players. "You pick up an instrument, you get a gig, you go to Europe—you know, this is life. . . . You're not going to tell me that somebody who picks up a trumpet in one year can learn a certain scale and go out there and try to improvise and people call him a musician. Nicholas [Payton] is a musician. Ellis [Marsalis] is a musician. Adonis Rose is a musician. I'm not tolerating that, man."[35] Likewise, Kidd Jordan later noted that these young bands, "whether in tune or not," were often lacking in the musical fundamentals.[36]

One new brass band that certainly does not fall into the category of the bands that Mayfield and Jordan were criticizing is the **New Orleans Nightcrawlers**. The band was founded in 1994 and made its public debut at Snug Harbor in November of that year. It was the idea of composer-arranger Tom McDermott (though there's no room for a piano in a brass band), trumpeter Kevin Clark, and bassist Matt Perrine. It began as something of a composers' workshop and played most of its gigs in clubs rather than in street parades. Leading to the formation of the band was

Scott Billington, the head of Rounder Records for whom the Dirty Dozen recorded (and eventually the 'Crawlers as well) asking McDermott do some arrangements for a recording by the Dozen. McDermott submitted an arrangement of "New Orleans Joys," which was used on the Dozen's 1993 recording, *Jelly*. They rejected another composition, "Heavy Henry" (inspired by Henry Butler). That led McDermott to look for a band to record it, hence the creation of the 'Crawlers, and, as it turned out, that tune was on their *Funknicity* CD, and Butler performed it.

Their first (self-titled) album appeared in 1996. As Tom McDermott wrote in the liner notes, the tunes were a mixture of originals (by McDermott, Leroy Jones, Stanton Moore, Rick Trolsen, Steve Masakowski, and Perrine) and "deconstructed standards"—all performed with a funky beat.

A second album (also on the Rounder label), *Funknicity*, came out the following year. The tunes are largely originals by band members, with more than one-third of them by Perrine, the band's music director at the time. This is a group of clearly talented players, composers, and arrangers. Though there is some variation in the eight to ten musicians who participated in these recordings, trumpeters Kevin Clark and Barney Floyd; saxophonists Eric Traub, Jason Mingledorff, and Ken "Snakebite" Jacobs; trombonist Craig Klein (Rick Trolsen would soon join him); and drummers Peter Kaplan and Frank Oxley were on both of them. Their music is brilliantly arranged, tightly presented, and all are good soloists.

The band became an almost immediate success, performing all over town and eventually touring in Europe, Latin America, and Asia. I would say that their style subsequently influenced several of the better neo–brass bands.

Another group formed during this decade was the **Pinettes**. They are of particular interest because they consisted only of young ladies, a first for New Orleans to my knowledge. In fact, they call themselves the world's only female brass band. The Original Pinettes started in 1991 (making a JazzFest appearance that very year) and, like so many of these new bands, was an outgrowth of a high-school band experience (in this case, St. Mary's Academy High School). Despite a fair bit of turnover in its personnel, its leader has always been snare drummer Christie Jourdain.[37] Their popularity remains intact to this day.

Finally, a word or two about a significant group that was formed during this decade: the **Black Men of Labor Social Aid and Pleasure Club**. Founded in 1994 by Fred Johnson, trumpeter Gregg Stafford and drummer Benny Jones Jr., the organization was inspired by and established following the death of Danny Barker. Barker did not want a jazz funeral because he was dismayed by the increasing amount of disrespect that had been displayed at such events in recent years. Fred Johnson remembered the evening that a group got together to try to persuade Blue Lu Barker to agree to a jazz funeral for her husband. "Well, Gregg stood up and said, 'Miss Lu, I'll make certain that the band will come in black and white [attire].' And I stood up on the other side of the room and said, 'Miss Lu, I'll make certain that we put 15 men in suits and ties to marshal the funeral.' When we did that, the music was so powerful that when we came out of the ceremony the guys said, 'We have to do this again.' And I said, 'Yeah, but not with a body.'"[38] And so the BMOL was born, and it continues to play an important role in the second-line parade scene and jazz scene in the city to this day.

And so the BMOL was born, and it continues to play an important role in the second-line parade scene and jazz scene in the city to this day. Dedicated to promoting the value of the arts and culture in the community, the group impresses with its creative formations and dancing to the music of traditional New Orleans jazz in its street performances.

SOME FINAL COMMENTS ABOUT THE '90S

A theory about ancient Greek history and civilization that had been building in academic circles at least since the previous decade, for reasons that are not entirely clear to me, seems to have reached a peak in the first half of the 1990s. It was termed "Afrocentrism," which (among other things) "claims that many of the great achievements of classical civilization were stolen from black Africa. It is the belief of Afrocentrists that

Greek philosophy and science were largely pilfered from African sources. A subsidiary claim is that many famous historical figures—Socrates and Cleopatra, for example—were black or at least partially black."[39] Obviously, I became aware of this point of view because of my own research in Greece and the Eastern Mediterranean. While it was not at all central to my own work, I felt obliged to examine at least some of the evidence that had been presented. I have to say—over all—that I found it quite unpersuasive.

The single publication that seems to have had most influence among the Afrocentrists was a book by Cornell scholar Martin Bernal, who had previously published mainly on Chinese and Southeast Asian history. The first volume of his longer work, *Black Athena: The Afroasiatic Roots of Classical Civilization*, appeared in the late '80s and was followed by other volumes. The most persuasive counter-arguments to Bernal were offered in two books by Wellesley classicist Mary Lefkowitz: *Not Out of Africa: How Afrocentrism Became an Excuse to Teach Myth as History* (1997) and *History Lesson* (2008). The ensuing issues were often not publicly addressed for obvious reasons, though they were hotly debated in private. As journalist John Leo noted, "I phoned seven Egyptologists and asked whether the ancient Egyptian population had been 'black.' Of course not, they all responded, but not for attribution, since, as one said, 'this subject is just too hot.'"[40]

But, of course, the Afrocentric point of view encompasses much larger terrain than just the classical world. Frankly, I made no effort to examine the evidence beyond that. In any case, I bring all of this up here because, at the very same time, the jazz world in the United States was embroiled in racist controversy—yet again. It was a controversy, as in the situation summarized above, about which many had opinions but few dared to express them publicly—at least initially. I observed (and heard) this thinking commonly among musicians in New Orleans, both black and white.

This particular phase of the controversy seems to have had its genesis in the '80s among white critics who were up in arms about Wynton Marsalis and his jazz programming at Lincoln Center, claiming that it gave disproportionate attention to black jazz musicians, that Marsalis was demonstrating a form of reverse racism ("Crow-Jimism"). The controversy came to a head with a debate between Marsalis and James Lincoln Collier, probably Marsalis's most severe critic, on August 7, 1994. The debate was attended by a loud standing-room-only audience in Lincoln Center's Kaplan Penthouse. The result of the head-to-head confrontation probably only exacerbated feelings on both sides and, in retrospect, probably did neither combatant any good. As one attendee observed, "such a public display of hostility benefits no one. Rather it does an injustice to the great American art form to which both Collier and Marsalis have devoted the better part of their lives."[41]

Yet the upshot of the debate had an effect on subsequent discussions of the state of jazz among musicians and others, not least in the birthplace of jazz itself. It also led to the publication of many books and articles on jazz and racism. *Jazz Times*, for example, devoted its March 1995 cover story to "Racism & Jazz, a reality check," with a lengthy article by black music writer James T. Jones IV.[42] At the end of the decade, the first major defense of white musicians against the criticism that jazz was black music that could only be played by black musicians was Richard M. Sudhalter's lengthy *Lost Chords: White Musicians and Their Contribution to Jazz, 1915–1945*. The book met with, expectably, mixed reviews. Critics objected to what they perceived to be a lack of balance in the book, suggesting that, among other things, the author was attacking the contributions of black musicians.[43]

Jazz writer and novelist Tom Piazza, who moved to New Orleans at about the time of the Great Debate, did a piece in the *New York Times* in January 1994 that, in my view, was a reasonable evaluation of the Lincoln Center squabble. "If [Lincoln Center's] program has anything resembling a tragic flaw, it is that its directorship has been tactless and defensive or worse, with some segments of the jazz press. . . . No program of this sort is perfect, and no administrator is without blind spots or prejudices. Jazz at Lincoln Center is important enough to argue over at length, but paranoia and ad hominem attacks do the music no good. Lincoln Center has a huge promise to fulfill, and anybody who loves jazz can only wish it well."

From my own experience talking with—and listening to—musicians on this subject, it is quite clear: there are many factors playing into their judgments, maybe most important of which would be equity in the workplace. After all, it is the availability of gigs that provides their livelihood. As for Wynton Marsalis, he was an incredibly talented and articulate young man—at the time, just in his early thirties. It is hard for me not to believe that there was a bit of envy and jealousy among his (often more senior) critics. And, obviously, many of them are white and he is black. Indeed, looking at this whole affair twenty years or so later makes me think somewhat of the treatment our president—Mr. Obama—is receiving at the hands of his political opponents today.

Marsalis, when asked in a 2012 interview what he learned from that "stormy period" in the '90s, replied, "For me, it wasn't that much of a storm. I was always around controversies since I first came out here [to the East Coast]. When you create change with your point of view, you have to be ready for what comes with that. And while they were [criticizing], there were also many people supporting and defending us, and putting money into what we were doing, and we *were* doing our thing: We put on thousands of concerts, hired thousands of musicians, sent out 80,000 Duke Ellington scores. We had 1700 educational events."[44]

Trumpeter and band leader Percy Humphrey was one of several pioneer jazzmen to pass away during the '90s. This is a view of the funeral cortege as it leaves Union Bethel Church on its way to the burial site in Mt. Olivet Cemetery. The Preservation Hall Jazz Band was on hand, and a large number of onlookers had been expected. The photograph gives some impression of the crowd that gathered for the occasion.

A number of the decade's young lions are seen in this 1999 band at the Maison Bourbon. *From left:* Louis Ford, clarinet; Stephen Walker, trombone; Mark Braud, trumpet; Leon Brown, trumpet; Mitchell Player, bass; and Julian Garcia, drums.

Jack Maheu, *left*, led the popular weekend jam sessions at Fritzel's on Bourbon Street. "The General," as he was often called by younger musicians, was a musical role model as well as a top-rated clarinetist. In this 1995 photo, he is seen listening (clearly with satisfaction) to one of his protégés, young Evan Christopher, take a solo.

Cornetist Chris Tyle led his popular Silver Leaf Jazz Band for a decade at the Can Can Café on Bourbon Street. Clarinetist Orange Kellin sits to the left of Tyle and pianist Steve Pistorius to the right.

A second-line parade, said to be the largest of its kind, marches down St. Peter Street from the French Quarter to Congo Square in conclusion of the Bechet Centennial, 1997. Leading the parade, *from the left,* are Bob Wilber, Fabrice Zammarchi, Walt Gower, Daniel Bechet (with sunglasses, no instrument, *at center*), Jim Galloway, Claude Luter, Jacques Gauthé, and Mike Owen.

Trumpeter Irvin Mayfield and Los Hombres Calientes appear at the 1999 opening of Storyville District on Bourbon Street. Seen here, *from the left,* are pianist Victor Atkins, bassist Peter Harris, Mayfield, and percussionists Yvette Bostic-Summers and Bill Summers. Drummer Jason Marsalis is obscured in the background.

Banu Gibson and her band at the Classic American Café on Decatur Street, 1999. *From the left,* Gibson, drummer Chris Tyle, clarinetist Tom Fischer, trumpeter Duke Heitger, and trombonist Mark Mullins. Gibson was part owner of this club, which unfortunately had only a brief life span.

Trombonist Steve Walker and his Swinging Six are shown here at Donna's Bar and Grill on North Rampart Street, 1998. *From the left,* pianist Jon Lefkoski, bassist Jason Stewart, Walker, trumpeter Irvin Mayfield, and (partially out of the picture) trumpeter Leon Brown. Not visible is drummer Dylan Hicks.

Frenchmen Street, ca. 1990. The Dream Palace is at the left, and Snug Harbor is barely visible in the next block on the left. Café Brasil is farther down the street on the right.

Nicholas Payton, *center*, appears at Sweet Lorraine's on St. Claude Avenue, 1999. At left is saxophonist Clarence Johnson III, and trumpeter Richwell Ison is at the right. Partially obscured in the background is bassist George French.

The French Quarter Festival in the 1990s. The composition of this band, *from the left*, is John Royen, piano; Jacques Gauthé, clarinet; Duke Heitger, trumpet; John Gill, banjo; Steve Yocum, trombone; and Tom Saunders, tuba.

Trumpeter Jimmy LaRocca, *center*, picked up where his father Nick left off with the Original Dixieland Jass Band (ODJB). Here the current ODJB performs at the French Quarter Festival in 1997. That's Jimmy's mom (and Nick's widow), Ruth LaRocca, dancing to her son's music. Band members include John Royen, piano; Tim Laughlin, clarinet; Mike Guma, trombone; and Dave Hansen, drums. The bassist is not recognizable.

Allison Miner, right, interviews Banu Gibson at JazzFest 1995. Miner died tragically just a few months later.

Doc Cheatham and Wynton Marsalis at the Louis Armstrong stamp celebration, 1995.

The Louis Armstrong U.S. postal stamp.

Doc Cheatham, with trumpet characteristically raised high, performs at his own postal cachet celebration at the Main Post Office, 1996. That's Mayor Marc Morial seated in the background to the left of Cheatham.

Doc Cheatham at a private party in the mid-1990s. Note the mute given him by King Oliver.

A portion of the large gathering that paid tribute to Doc Cheatham in St. Peter's Church in New York City in June 1997.

Daniel Bechet, *right*, the son of Sidney, and Jacques Gauthé at the Sidney Bechet Celebration, 1997.

The late jazz historian and archivist Dick Allen, with Andrea DuPlessis, at a private party in the 1990s.

Andrea DuPlessis, George Hocutt, and Jerry Brock, co-producers of the Grammy-winning *Doc Cheatham & Nicholas Payton* CD, have a committee meeting at Snug Harbor, 1996.

Doc Cheatham and Nicholas Payton exchange smiles during a break in the recording studio, 1994.

Christina Machado in the Parlor Room at Storyville District, 1999. Drummer Adonis Rose is in the background.

The New Orleans Nightcrawlers manage to squeeze onto the small stage at Snug Harbor for their February 1995 gig. *From the left,* Eric Traub, Snakebite Jacobs, Evan Christopher, Matt Perrine, Barney Floyd, Mark Morris, Kevin Clark, Rick Trolsen, and Craig Klein. Percussionist Pete Kaplan is obscured by Trolsen.

Don Vappie, *left*, and his Creole Jazz Serenaders at JazzFest 1999. Visible in this photograph are Tom Fischer, clarinet; Jamil Sharif, trumpet; Mark Chatters, trumpet; and Alonzo Bowens, tenor saxophone. The rhythm section is not visible.

Legendary Buddy Bolden, "the first man of jazz," never received a proper burial. Accordingly, a memorial marker was erected in his honor in Holt Cemetery (where he was known to have been buried) in September 1997. Gertrude Bolden Tucker, Buddy's granddaughter, was flown down from Chicago for the celebration. She is seen here modeling a commemorative Bolden T-shirt.

This marvelous clarinet mural adorning the Holiday Inn on South Rampart Street was dedicated in May 1997. The work of Louisiana artist Robert Dafford, the mural later served as a useful focal point for the annual meetings of the International Clarinet Association held in New Orleans. The mural has become a local landmark.

Gayle Hazelwood was appointed by the National Park Service as superintendent of the Jazz National Historical Park in 1998. Under her leadership, the Jazz Park began to flourish in the following decade. Hazelwood is here illustrating her plans for the proposed park to be located within the confines of Louis Armstrong Park.

5
Epilogue
SOME FINAL THOUGHTS

Looking back over the decades just surveyed, one might ask if any general trends are apparent. What, for example, can we say about the makeup of the jazz audience during that period?

On a national level, the surveys of the National Endowment for the Arts indicate a gradual increase in the percentage of adults attending jazz performances through the last three decades of the twentieth century. Likewise, they point to an increase, decade by decade, from 1982 onward among adults thirty-five years of age and older. Yet, for adults between eighteen and thirty-four, there was a consistent *decline*. The statistics also suggest that, the more education the listener had, the more disposed he/she would be toward jazz music.[1] It would be interesting to know precisely the extent to which the clear increase in jazz education throughout the country correlated with those results. For example, to what extent is the size of the jazz audience affected by the increased number of schools teaching jazz courses? Unfortunately, to my knowledge, we do not have that information. And, of course, there is no information about the audience's preference for modern jazz vs. more traditional jazz styles. We cannot assume, I believe, that every jazz fan will appreciate all styles of jazz. (OKOMists take note.)

In New Orleans, the picture is even less clear—at least quantitatively. We do know that festival attendance at both the Jazz and Heritage Festival and French Quarter Festival was on a noticeably upward trajectory during the last decades of the century. My guess would be that that is a reflection of the increased diversity of the musical offerings at the two festivals, thus attracting a larger and more diverse audience. While there are no published figures (as far as I am aware) to indicate the relative numbers of people attending concerts of jazz, pop, R&B, gospel, and other musical styles, my *impression* would be that the pop offerings at

JazzFest were more widely attended than the jazz offerings (trad and mod combined) and that attendance in the Jazz Tent (generally more modern) outnumbered that in the Economy Hall Tent (more traditional). In the earliest decades of the French Quarter Festival, however, the organizers seem to have shown more interest in the traditional jazz styles. Later on, however, the FQF has become increasingly diverse.

There is pretty clearly a generational difference between those listening to modern jazz as opposed to those who prefer the more traditional styles. That is quite evident by visually comparing the audiences in the Economy Hall Tent with those in the Jazz Tent at JazzFest. It is also suggested by those who choose to attend the Nickel-a-Dance soirees, and one need only check out those listening to the various trad bands on Bourbon Street during the FQF. New Orleans's reputation as the birthplace of jazz continued to draw visitors—both foreign and domestic—to the city. I would hasten to add that these age differences *do not mean* that the older folks listen only to trad and never to more modern styles. At the same time, it is always heartening for me to see a steady stream of younger folks listening to both styles of jazz (contrary, perhaps, to the national trend). This became especially apparent to me during the swing-dance craze of the '90s (and beyond). They tended to bring a more youthful profile to the audiences, and to the musicians as well.

In this connection, I asked two officers—Ian Thiele and Lee Goode—of the International Association of Jazz Record Collectors at their 2012 meeting in New Orleans about the age profile of their membership. Both seemed to agree that the average age would be between sixty-five and seventy, but their musical tastes are wide-ranging. Goode said that the youngest was born in 1991 and the oldest in 1917. While this twenty-first-century data may not seem relevant to the later twentieth century, my guess would be that the IAJRC age profile hasn't changed much over the years.[2]

I am equally encouraged to see more young people daring to go into jazz music as a profession. That is reflected in large measure by the growing number of jazz education programs, both in the city and across the country. It is a risky business, and their choice is certainly not made for financial reasons. Like so many artistic endeavors, however, it must be made out of love for the music. To which I say, "Bravo!"

Yet as I write this in 2013, I am gaining an impression that many young people are not particularly interested in becoming identified as "jazz fans" in the same way as perhaps earlier generations were—which, of course, is not to say that they have no interest in what we would call jazz. While they happily attend jazz performances, their stylistic preferences may not be so firmly fixed and their musical tastes may be rather more wide-ranging. It seems clear, in any case, that the musical tastes of young people have had a significant effect on the present jazz "brand" at least since the 1970s. I think that trend will surely continue.

I would suggest, in short, that JazzFest, with its large annual attendance numbers, would provide a good laboratory to conduct a demographic survey addressing some of the issues raised above. Though more difficult to carry out, a comparable survey at the FQF would also be of interest. I would guess that the benefits of these results would be useful to more than just the local music community.

While there is always grumbling about pay, it is a truism that many local jazz musicians are totally supported by their music (including, of course, record sales). There are those who say, in fact, that the work opportunities for jazz musicians here are better than in much larger cities such as New York or Los Angeles. In an interview in 2003, drummer Trevor Richards emphasized, "The fact is that New Orleans does offer the most [work] opportunities of any city that I know in the United States."[3]

Nevertheless, a large number of New Orleans musicians are unable to afford health insurance (a problem that goes well beyond the music industry in this country, unfortunately). To counteract that, the **New Orleans Musicians' Clinic** (NOMC) was founded in 1998. It is a wonderful organization that has helped countless musicians in various ways. Their current mission statement reads in part as follows.[4] The NOMC "is dedicated to keeping New Orleans' performers alive in body, mind, and spirit by providing comprehensive health care and mental health/social services. As the 'medical home' for more than 2,400 local musicians and tradition bearers, the NOMC's Culture of Caring Model provides cost-efficient access to high quality healthcare and wellness programs for our patients, regardless of their ability to pay."[5] I know many musicians who have taken advantage of the services provided by the NOMC, and therefore I am pleased to support their work on a regular basis.

One local musician remarked to me: "Most of the full-time professional musicians I know are reliant on the Musicians' Clinic, unless they have wives with full-time jobs and a health plan they can get on. The lack of health care is, of course, the great festering sore on the American visage, and it is particularly acute among musicians. Even high-profile jazz musicians are often without coverage because the cost of private plans is simply prohibitive unless you're wealthy, which very, very few jazz musicians are. I'm often amazed by how much money non-musicians *think* I make playing music. People think high visibility—fame, in other words—automatically equals wealth. Me, I remember that Anita O'Day finished her life living in a trailer and was very nearly killed off by charity hospital treatment.[6]

"As to the notion that New Orleans has more gigs than any other North American city," the local musician continued, "I'd have to say that's true. There's a lot of work . . . , but not much money. So, it's possible to work seven days a week, as I have in the past, and still take home less than $35,000 a year. It's a mixed blessing."

Turning to another topic, it is in fact one that has bothered me since moving to New Orleans permanently. As a one-time resident of Nashville—"Music City USA" (as it was known when I lived there)—I always felt that that was a misnomer because of the restricted nature of the music that dominated the city. "Country Music Capital," I thought, would have been a much more appropriate epithet. It seemed that New Orleans, with its diversity of music, would fit the title of "Music City" much more appropriately.

And then came Austin, the "Live Music Capital of the World." This seems to be the current official slogan for the city, but again—in my experience—its music scene is rather more limited than that of New Orleans, and I cannot imagine that it has more live music venues per capita than the Crescent City. (Still, I did meet a couple of young musicians from there at FQF in 2011, who spoke glowingly of the incipient trad jazz scene in Austin.)

My question, I guess, is, what is the musical slogan of our city? Yes, unofficially, it is known as the birthplace of jazz, but I don't see this much trumpeted about by the local tourist organizations or the Chamber of Commerce. It almost seems to be an embarrassment to the city's public relations establishment—though the word "jazz" is frequently seen in blatantly *nonmusical* contexts about town. That, in my view, is due in large measure to officialdom's profound ignorance of jazz. (Or is political correctness a more important factor?) Rather, we're known as "The Big Easy," at best, but more often simply as a place to party and get sloshed—*Laissez les bon temps rouler.* We see signs on Bourbon Street announcing places to get "big ass beers." That certainly makes me proud to be a New Orleanian!

As I have indicated elsewhere, cluelessness about jazz is shockingly widespread in this city—of all places. We have read and heard repeatedly in statements by musicians and other members of the music community that New Orleanians lack an interest in jazz. That this mindset exists in high places in the city's promotional hierarchy is particularly disturbing since those are the places that set the tone for the city's reputation in the outside world. In my opinion, the only mayor of the city in the twentieth century to show something of an understanding of jazz was Marc Morial. He was visible at many major musical events and seems to have acknowledged the importance of jazz to the city. In 2001, at the renaming of the airport, he went so far as to call Louis Armstrong "the greatest New Orleanian of all."

My wish, in short, is that those who promote the city become more intimately familiar with the role in the city's history that jazz has played, and continues to play, and that, somehow, they will take that into account in their promotion of New Orleans. Where is the *official* slogan that reflects this?

••••••••••••••••••••••••

By the end of the last century I had been living permanently in New Orleans for about a decade. Given my listening (and playing) predilection for early jazz since my teenage years, I had been enjoying—on virtually a daily basis—attending live performances of the best traditional (in the broad sense of the word) jazz bands in the city along with some of the best such players from elsewhere who visited New Orleans. Most of those players were top-notch, highly skilled and often well-educated musically. But they were playing a repertoire that I had been listening to for decades, and I was beginning to tire of hearing it over and over. I had begun to wonder how such skilled musicians could do that day after day and still retain their sanity and/or self-respect. I talked with many of them about that, and most had the same response (to paraphrase), "It's a living. We're playing what the audiences want to hear." That's the price to pay for playing to a market based on tourism (including what I call OKOMists from all over the world). Those visitors come to the city—the birthplace of jazz—to hear the music for which the city is famous and they are most familiar with—and, of course, one can't blame them for that. (Yet even many of them were beginning to complain by that time that there was not enough such music to be heard in town.) Just think, in this connection, of the sign prominently displayed on the wall behind the bandstand at Preservation Hall that read, essentially, "Requests $1.00–$2.00, The SAINTS $5.00." (Inflation has now raised the cost of "the Saints" to $20.00!) The good musicians always played "The Saints Go Marching In" for their audiences but, privately, they regularly complained about having to do so.

But some of the best of them had begun to deal with their frustrations in a variety of creative ways. I began to notice this in the 1990s when, for example, trumpeters like Nicholas Payton and Leroy Jones recorded CDs (both in 1996, as it happened)—Payton's *Gumbo Nouveau* and Jones's *Props for Pops*—that included many of the traditional evergreens—but played in more untraditional styles. I found that very refreshing.

Another way of coping was for the musicians themselves to compose new music, sometimes in a variety of styles. Ragtime pianist Tom McDermott recorded a CD in that same year (1996) that I consider a brilliant collection of original compositions in *all twenty-four major and minor keys*. It's called *All the Keys and Then Some*. The pianist wrote in his liner notes, "Musicians, especially those who play in only one idiom, tend to play in the same handful of keys their whole lives. Playing in one of the lesser-used keys, G-sharp minor for instance, is a bit like visiting a cousin you knew existed but had never bothered to get to know. All the keys are interrelated, of course, so any foray into even the most remote key will add to your knowledge of the ones familiar to you." The approach of the album was part of a venerable tradition in classical music, but I found it, once again, a breath of fresh air on the local music scene.

Another example of new music composed by someone associated with the traditional style could be heard in the work of clarinetist Tim Laughlin, who began writing and recording his own tunes in the mid-'90s. His album—again in the year 1996—*Blue Orleans* on the Good Time Jazz label became a big success in the local jazz community, especially his original title track. The instrumental configuration on that track was unexpected and unique to this recording. Besides the clarinetist, the ensemble consisted of two trumpets (Kevin Clark and Connie Jones), two trombones (Al Barthlow and Mike Genevay, the latter on bass trombone), a tenor saxophonist (Tony Dagradi, normally considered a modernist), David Torkanowsky (not normally regarded as a traditionalist) at the Hammond B-3 organ, guitarist Hank Mackie, Matt Perrine (on electric rather than acoustic bass), and Johnny Vidacovich on drums. The ten-piece unit produced the sound of a big band that, given the funky work of Dagradi and Torkanowsky, was at variance with the standard small-ensemble New Orleans trad sound. It was new and fresh. A second original on that CD, "King of the Mardi Gras," also had a fresh approach and became an immediate favorite during Carnival season. Another ten-piece ensemble piece, it was distinguished by the use of *three* trombones (David Sager added to Barthlow and Genevay). But the second-line drumming of Reed Vaughan along with Matt Perrine's sousaphone gave the tune a real (though more arranged) brass-band feel. All in all, this recording represented something of a departure for Laughlin and pointed him in a more creative direction, which he continued to pursue in subsequent decades.

But there were many others in the local traditional jazz community that were also breaking with the tradition. To name just some of them: Jimmy LaRocca (who claims to have written hundreds, if not thousands, of original melodies), other Nightcrawlers' sidemen apart from McDermott like Matt Perrine and Rick Trolsen, and clarinetist Dr. Michael

White. All display their originality on recordings while continuing to perform the trad standards in their live gigs. All of which suggests that the future of traditional jazz—in New Orleans, at least—is quite secure.

I would conclude by noting that the tourists still come to New Orleans to hear traditional jazz, but perhaps to a lesser extent R&B and modern jazz. It would be very interesting to know to what extent these other musical genres draw visitors to the city.

NOTES

PREFACE

1. I will never forget, however, one autograph that I secured some years later. My wife, children, and I were in the Minneapolis airport preparing to fly to Greece for a sabbatical year in 1973–74. As we were standing around talking with other family members before boarding the plane, I spotted an old man slumped over on a seat nearby. I thought to myself, "My God, that's Duke Ellington!" His had always been (and still is) my favorite big band. I had seen and heard the band live several times by that time, but I'd never been that close to the great man himself. I didn't want to disturb him since he didn't look well, but I couldn't resist. I walked over to him, introduced myself, and asked if he would sign a piece of paper (a sheet from my mother's check register was all we could dig up quickly), which of course he kindly did. (I still have it somewhere.) That was in the spring of 1973. Duke Ellington died almost exactly one year later, when we were still in Greece. Very sad. As my onetime colleague at Indiana University, David Baker, used to say, Ellington was the "Mt. Olympus" of jazz composers.

2. My wife Kathryn and I had been married for nearly twenty-two years at that point. She was the mother of my two children, Mark, age fifteen, who was born in Greece, and Kirsten, age eleven, at the time of their mother's death.

3. My decision to retire early from academe was based, in large part, upon a desire to live a more "normal" lifestyle. My life for the previous three decades had been intensely "workaholic," with little time left to pursue worthwhile personal interests beyond teaching and research. Call it "burnout" perhaps, but I needed time to rediscover myself. Moreover, I had come to the conclusion that higher education was no longer what it had been when I started out. I did not like what I perceived to be the "corporate" mentality that had increasingly come to characterize university life, not—I hasten to add—just at my own university.

I had completed my doctorate in classical archaeology at the University of Pennsylvania in 1964. Upon receiving that degree, I took a position at Vanderbilt University, where I remained until accepting an offer to move to Indiana University in 1966. I stayed at IU for twenty-six years, founding and directing the graduate program in classical archaeology from 1970 to 1985 and serving as chair of the Department of Classical Studies for the three years just prior to my wife's death. I opted for early retirement in 1992. Apart from my teaching and administrative responsibilities, I spent all of those twenty-six years at IU involved in excavation, fieldwork, and research in Greece, where I directed the excavations at the major prehistoric site of Franchthi Cave from 1967 to 1997. I was general editor of (as well as contributor to) the multivolume series *Excavations at Franchthi Cave, Greece* (Bloomington: Indiana University Press, 1987–93). When I retired, I was named professor emeritus of classical studies.

During a sabbatical year (1980–81) as special research fellow at the American School of Classical Studies in Athens, I found time to collect data that led to the first publication in English of a short history of jazz in Greece (1987). Soon thereafter, even before retiring from Indiana, I began contributing to *JazzTimes* magazine during the editorship of W. Royal Stokes. After moving to New Orleans, I began writing for *The Mississippi Rag*, doing a monthly column as well as periodic feature articles, in 1995 and continued doing so until the publication ceased to exist due to the death of the publisher in 2008. I have been writing for *The Clarinet* from 1998 to the present, serving on the editorial staff as a jazz columnist and feature writer. I have also contributed jazz pieces to a variety of other magazines and newspapers. I began a website devoted to New Orleans jazz in 2010 (www.neworeleansnotes.com) and published my first book on a jazz subject the following year: *Traditional New Orleans Jazz: Conversations with the Men Who Make the Music* (2011).

4. As I was writing this, a national study revealed that Louisiana has the sixth-highest income inequality in the country (nola.com, November 15, 2012). The report, which was put out by the Center on Budget and Policy Priorities and the Economic Institute in Washington, D.C., "tracks inequality from the late 1970s, a time period chosen because it represents the end of a pattern that began in the 1950s and saw all income levels increase."

5. A series of surveys by the National Endowment for the Arts showed that, in 1982, less than 10 percent of the U.S. adult population attended jazz performances. The "highly dedicated jazz audience," however, was only about 3 percent of the adult population. See Baker, ed., 1990, 1–8. Additional NEA surveys have been conducted in 1992, 2002, and 2008. They seem to show the situation getting worse with the passage of time. The rate of change for college-educated adult attendance at jazz events between 1982 and 2008 fell by 23 percent (*Arts Participation 2008, Highlights from a National Survey* [Washington, D.C.: National Endowment for the Arts, 2009]).

6. Versatile local pianist David Torkanowsky, who plays everything from trad to free-form jazz, has said that trad is not a style as much as an "attitude."

I continue to use the increasingly (it seems) denigrated four-letter word "jazz"—or as New Orleans–born Nicholas Payton termed it "J***." Payton, however, really prefers the term "BAM" (an acronym for "Black American Music"). Indeed, he is considered—or considers himself—the father of the BAM movement, which had become a hot subject of debate and controversy on the internet as I was writing this.

7. I had the good fortune of traveling as a jazz journalist to Cuba for two weeks in the spring of 2001. I recounted my journey in two brief publications (Jacobsen 2001 and 2002). It was an absolutely wonderful experience, and, when our country finally relaxes

(as it now seems to be doing gradually) its misguided view toward that island nation, I recommend a trip there most highly. (I should probably add that, as I write this, Cuba itself seems to be relaxing its formerly rigid stance toward its own expatriate musicians.) Unfortunately, I have yet to visit the vast country of Brazil. But I am making plans to do so in the near future. Fortunately, I have the advice and guidance at my disposal of a number of fine New Orleans musicians who have often performed there and know the country well. I have, in fact, made it a point to visit as many of the Caribbean nations as possible, given their traditionally close ties with New Orleans (which has been considered by many as the northernmost outpost of the Caribbean).

1. PROLOGUE: THE 1960S

1. The Beatles seem to have made a single memorable visit to New Orleans in September 1964. They performed before a crowd of (reportedly) thousands of nearly hysterical fans at what is now known as Tad Gormley Stadium in City Park.

2. The original was published in 1961. A new edition was issued in 2005. See note 3, below.

3. These observations, excerpted from their book, appear in Claxton and Berendt 2005, 44–53. Suhor would undoubtedly disagree with their conclusion here. In a paper delivered at the IAJRC convention in New Orleans in September 2012 entitled "Jazzmen and Strippers in Postwar New Orleans," Suhor emphasized the correlation between modern jazz players and strip clubs. He said that the latter served as home for most of the modernists. That "pit band bonanza," as he called it, lasted until about 1964. See also Suhor 2001, 234–50.

4. The strip-club scene on Bourbon Street at this time is well illustrated in a short documentary film produced and directed by Peggy Scott Laborde, *Bourbon Street: The Neon Strip*, that aired locally on WYES-TV in 1993 (and is still available on DVD). It makes reference to and shows clips from the Brinkley program, for which the highly respected Dick Allen of the Tulane Jazz Archive was a consultant. Allen later said, "People resented it [Brinkley's comments] tremendously because it made it seem as if there wasn't much jazz here." In answer to a follow-up question, however, Allen admitted that there really hadn't been much good jazz.

5. Suhor 2001, 151.

6. Ibid., 237. According to Suhor, "The positive side of the crackdown was that some former strip club owners decided to offer music (not necessarily jazz) as the main entertainment fare." He concludes, "To paraphrase Mark Twain, the death of stripping was greatly exaggerated; but the musical climate that had been growing since 1959 with Fountain, Hirt, Preservation Hall, and the Playboy was further enhanced by Garrison's high profile operation."

7. Ibid., 294–98.

8. Sancton 2012, 1–2. For a history of Preservation Hall, see Carter 1991.

9. Sancton 2012, 3.

10. Martyn had, in fact, been preceded by the ill-fated trumpeter Ken Colyer, who came to New Orleans in the early '50s. He is said to have been "the first professional English musician to play publicly and record with black New Orleans musicians. The story of his being jailed and deported after outstaying his dubious welcome by the white authorities elevated him to the status of a guru" (Wood 2000, vol. 1: 116). Accordingly, a group of devoted acolytes formed the Ken Colyer Trust, and they continue to make annual pilgrimages to New Orleans.

11. Darnell 1976, 3.

12. The collection has obviously experienced a somewhat challenging history. More recently, the museum suffered considerable damage from Hurricane Katrina. Having been closed to the public since 2005, it has now been renovated and partially opened once again in 2011. As of this writing, the date of the complete opening has yet to be announced. For a history of the Jazz Museum through its first half century, see Don Marquis 1996–97.

13. Deano Assunto, the son of Frankie Assunto, has compiled a collection of still pictures and video clips of the original band on DVD, including some of the 1950s Ed Sullivan shows. It is not as yet available commercially, but he can be contacted about it at deanoassunto@dukesofdixieland.com.

14. Jacobsen 2011, 119–20.

15. Feather 1966; Feather and Gitler 1976.

16. The most complete and up-to-date account of Armstrong and the All Stars (and his later years in general) is Ricky Riccardi's *What a Wonderful World* (2011).

17. Darnell 1978, 3–9. Jones was awarded an honorary degree by Loyola University in 2012. Thanks to Connie for his comments to me about Teagarden's last days.

I would also add these comments about Jones given me by Pete Fountain in January 2004: "Connie and I go back a long way. I was the best man at his wedding nearly 50 years ago. Really I wasn't the 'best man,' I was just there. Connie is one in a million. I would compare him to [cornetist] Bobby Hackett. He plays like an angel, and I have told him that. He played with me for 15–16 years, in what we called the 'big little band.' He was playing trumpet then. Connie is a helluva gentleman—never says anything bad about anyone. He just plays his horn."

18. Brinkman and Abrams 2011, 115.

19. Pers. comm., March 2013.

20. Suhor 2001, 242.

21. Belletto, pers. comm., February 23, 2012.

22. Kolb 2012, 61.

23. Ibid.

24. Battiste is the subject of a recent autobiography, *Unfinished Blues* (2010), by Battiste with Celestan, 2010.

25. Feather 1960, 50.

26. Suhor 2001, 75–97. Jazz writer and one-time New Orleans resident Doug Ramsey (2011) puts it this way: "JazzFest, as it was christened at its birth in the late 1960s, began as the purest of jazz festivals, integrated with a judicious smattering of associated events involving Louisiana food and culture. The 1968 and '69 festivals, along with certain years at Newport and Monterey, were among the music's milestone large events. They were not big money makers and they did not fit some New Orleans movers' and shakers' vision of what a festival should be in a city whose motto is 'Let The Good Times Roll.' . . . The focus was on jazz and its central role in the history and life of the city." Suhor (2001, 35–37) also discusses pre-1968 attempts at organizing "large-scale jazz festivals." All failed to be fulfilled.

27. Dr. Charles Chamberlain of the Louisiana State Museum gave a lecture in April 2008 entitled "Sharing the Stage: Inter-racial Jazz and Civil Rights in New Orleans, 1946–1970." He stated, "While jazz in New Orleans is often viewed as good-time party music, during the 1940s and early 1950s interracial jazz performances emerged as a form of protest to racial segregation among some musicians and promoters. Reacting to this issue, the state legislature passed a law in 1956 prohibiting 'inter-racial entertainments,' a move that prompted Louis Armstrong and his integrated All-Stars to stay away from Louisiana until 1965. Despite the new law, white and black musicians still found ways to share their music, and this cooperation laid the foundation for the modern music industry in New Orleans." The law was officially termed "Revised Statute 4.451." Because he and his band were not allowed to perform in 1949 in the Municipal Auditorium, as Chamberlain also notes, Armstrong vowed not to be buried in the city—just one of many tragedies associated with him in this city. Armstrong's boycott lasted from 1956 to 1965.

28. See, for example, the comments of Clive Wilson and Trevor Richards on this subject in Jacobsen 2011, 182–83 and 206–7.

2. JAZZ IS BACK: THE 1970S

1. Trumpeter Clive Wilson, personal communication, December 8, 2011.

2. Morgenstern 1977, 44.

3. Saal and Kuflik 1977, 50.

4. Riccardi 2011, 300–301.

5. Ibid., 302.

6. Suhor 2001, 98.

7. Ibid.

8. Suhor 2001, 100.

9. Thanks to the research of the late Tad Jones (1953–2007), it is now quite widely agreed that Armstrong's birth date was August 4, 1901, rather than, as the trumpeter himself would say, July 4, 1900.

10. Ms. Catlett passed away in April 2012, just days before her ninety-seventh birthday—and about a month after ace jazz bassist/composer Rufus Reid appeared at Louisiana State University in Baton Rouge to premier his new composition, *Quiet Pride*, which was inspired by the work of Catlett. Reid, who called the artist "a national treasure," also performed at the Old Mint and the New Orleans Center for the Creative Arts on March 1, 2012. Catlett did numerous other works of art for the city, including the statue of Mahalia Jackson in Armstrong Park and a wonderful JazzFest poster depicting a graceful Afro-Caribbean dancer.

11. For accounts about Armstrong Park and the statue, see Feather 1976, 19–21; Floyd Levin 1976, 16–19.

12. Wood 1976, 17–21. Another piece that does something of the same, though perhaps more professionally, is Suhor 1975, 73–77.

13. For more on Belletto in this decade, see Spedale 1984, 103–10. Many thanks, too, to Al himself (whose health is fragile currently) and Linda Rhodes for their personal recollections and communications.

14. Kolb 2012, 61.

15. I had a number of brief conversations with Finola over the years, but never a true interview (though I tried more than once). He resisted that for some reason. He would say something like, "You can write whatever you want when I'm gone." As his friend Will Severns confided (pers. comm., January 2003), "George was so funny about such things. As far as his career was concerned, he could be his own worst enemy sometimes." He was a very bright man with wide-ranging interests, one of which was eastern Mediterranean archaeology. Ironically, we shared archaeological friends/colleagues in Chicago.

A brief contemporary account of Finola and his music was done by Owen "Duke" Darnell (1976, 3–5). Darnell also has some interesting comments about the city's jazz scene in the mid-seventies: "New Orleans is a place where jazz musicians congregate and can make a living playing their music." As we know, that is by no means the case in most places. Later, he adds, "It is the only city in the world where the jazz buff on any night of the week can pick and choose among several good traditional jazz bands." Those observations—pretty much—have held true right down to the present.

16. Marquis 2010, 25–26; Suhor 1975, 74.

17. The liner notes of the Dukes' 2006 album, *Timeless*, explains the story in part: "Back in late 1974, John Shoup, a television producer for PBS and later The Discovery Channel who also managed and produced many artists, flew out to Las Vegas to meet with musician/singer Louis Prima at Prima's golf course. Shoup wanted Prima's permission to take over his lease at the Monteleone Hotel's rooftop nightclub in New Orleans' French Quarter. Two months later, on New Year's Eve, December 31, 1974, Shoup opened 'Dukes Place' atop the Monteleone. It featured the home of the newest ensemble of THE DUKES of Dixieland, with Connie Jones as leader."

Another account of the transition from the original Dukes to the Dukes of the John Shoup era, along with a history of the band to 1984, is given by Spedale (1984, 135ff.).

Jones stayed with the band for only a year or so and was replaced by Mike Vax as leader. A fine reed player, Otis Bazoon, was in that band and became its leader before the end of the decade. And so it went for many years, until the late Richard "Dickie" Taylor (1940–2010) took over the leadership of the band in 1990. But that is only the beginning. The checkered history of the later Dukes, which has had several incarnations and personnel changes over the years, has included a long legal battle with the Assunto family that has yet to be fully resolved as of this writing.

18. From the author's interview with Royen conducted in July 1998. For the full story, see Jacobsen 2011, 134. Ewell, then in his sixties, stayed in town for only a relatively short time before moving to Florida—though he did return to New Orleans for recording sessions and the like a number of times thereafter.

19. Belletto, pers. comm., March 2, 2012.

20. Spedale 1984, 105–6. Lu and Charlie's closed in 1978, according to Lu herself. (See also Lichtenstein and Dankner 1993, 242–43, where the closing is dated to 1977.) Charlie Bering went on in 1979 to become the producer of the night concerts for JazzFest for a time. He opened a large and impressive club—Charlie B's—on Convention Center Boulevard in the early 1990s. It hosted some great national touring groups, but, unfortunately, it did not last more than a couple of years.

21. For more on Lu & Charlie's, see David Lasocki's 2004 interview with Lula Lowe Lewis (Lasocki 2012, 29–37). "We were like the beginning of a new era of jazz in New Orleans," she said.

22. See www.crescentpalmsmotel.com.

23. For much more about Astral Project, see the remarkable book by Lasocki (2012).

24. Suhor 2001, 97. See also chapter 1, n. 26, above.

25. See Smith 1991. A handy but not entirely reliable source (there are some glaring errors in the jazz coverage) for the early years of JazzFest in particular is McCaffrey 2005. But, as that source notes and I note elsewhere, JazzFest records are "spotty" at best, especially for the early years. Suhor has been one of the most vociferous in contesting the 1970 edition as the first. In addition to the 1968 and 1969 festivals, he suggests that there were even earlier possible prototypes (1995, 11ff).

26. Spedale 1984, 105. Which festivals Belletto specifically had a hand in are not specified.

27. McCaffrey 2005, 50.

28. Ibid., 58.

29. Ibid., 78. According to Matt Goldman, longtime press and advertising director for the festival, who adds, "no one really kept numbers" at that time. See also Smith 1991, 21. Goldman later added, "I don't have a good place to send you for additional attendance numbers as prior to 1985 there aren't good records" (pers. comm., March 23, 2012).

30. Indeed, a number of European jazz festivals have been devoted especially to New Orleans jazz, and hundreds of New Orleans musicians have been invited to perform at those events over the years. To name just a few that I have had the good fortune of attend-

ing: New Orleans Jazz Ascona, in lovely Ascona (on the shores of Lake Maggiore), Switzerland, which has been running annually since 1974; Molde International Jazz Festival in Molde, Norway, since 1961 and one of Europe's oldest (Uncle Lionel Batiste served as grand marshal for the festival's jazz parade for many years until his death in 2012); and *Sildajazz* ("Herring Jazz") in Haugesund, Norway (continuously since 1987). While New Orleans musicians still play a big role in those festivals, their programs—like here in New Orleans—seem to have become more eclectic in recent years. The Swiss festival has even modified its name to the simpler "JazzAscona Festival" by dropping the "New Orleans" component of its title.

31. McCaffrey 2005, 70–73.

32. Smith 1991, 74.

33. This was written in 1972 but never published. Don generously shared his notes with me in March 2012, for which I sincerely thank him.

34. The others are located in New York City, San Francisco, San Pedro/Los Angeles, Miami, and Houston. The New York church was established in 1878, thus making it the oldest of the missions still in existence.

35. Some of the above narrative has been taken from my brief obituary of Narvin Kimball in the periodic publication of the New Orleans church, *Gulfposten*, by the author (2006, 6), along with my liner notes for the church's excellent centennial CD, *Jazzkirken: 100 Years in New Orleans* (2006). The latter is a compilation of music by some of the many bands that performed in the church over the years and is still available for purchase at the church. I also wish to thank Mr. Bengt Andersson, a member of the Seamen's Church and former board member of the New Orleans Jazz Club, for his help in compiling a list of bands that have performed there since the 1970s.

36. Hasse quoted in Herzig 2011, 239. In my opinion, there is a fine line distinguishing between repertory and "ghost" bands such as the Glenn Miller Orchestra led by Buddy DeFranco, the Tommy Dorsey band led by Buddy Morrow, the Count Basie Orchestra led by Frank Foster or Bill Hughes, or even the Mercer Ellington Orchestra.

37. Ray 2012.

38. Herzig 2011, 309.

39. White 2010, 2–20.

40. Ibid., 3.

41. Ibid., 7.

42. Ibid., 15.

43. Ibid.

44. Ibid., 19; Burns 2006, 13–61; Jacobsen 2011, 66–109.

45. Jacobsen and Marquis 2006 (May), 2–4.

46. This conclusion clearly contradicts the following statement: "In 1972, Fairview pastor Rev. Andrew Darby approached Danny to form a youth brass band affiliated with the church; the stated aim was to keep the youngsters off the streets" (Burns 2006, 15).

47. Lucien's father, Charles Sr., assisted Barker in managing the band. The Barbarin

family was one of the most influential musically in the city, and Danny Barker considered himself part of the Barbarin clan. His grandfather was multi-instrumentalist Isidore Barbarin, and his uncles were the great drummers Paul and Louis Barbarin.

48. Jacobsen and Marquis 2006 (May): 4. Michael White joined later, being a part of what he calls the "second generation" of the band.

49. Jacobsen 2011, 78–79.

50. Ibid., 78ff. This interview was conducted in 2004. The name "Hurricane" came from Danny Barker, according to Jones. Speaking about the Fairview band, Barker said, "he wanted to call us the Hurricane Band 'because when you come up the street you all blow like a hurricane.'"

51. Burns 2006, 69ff.

52. Lichtenstein and Dankner 1993, 237–39.

53. Burns 2006, 71.

54. Herzig 2011, 101.

55. Suhor 2001, 71–74.

56. I owe a debt of thanks to both Professors Hebert and Mahoney for taking the time to share details about the early history of jazz studies at their university.

57. Kennedy (2002, 82–128) has provided a detailed account of the long and complex process of creating the New Orleans Center for the Creative Arts. In addition, Kennedy's book is a valuable source for understanding the important contributions to the training of future New Orleans jazz musicians by many fine public-school music teachers such as Yvonne Busch.

I also want to thank Mr. Matt Hassebrock, librarian at NOCCA's John Breaux Library, for kindly providing much helpful information about the early days of the school.

Mention should perhaps be made of the "Jazz Workshop," a short-lived program for children started by respected saxophonist Earl Turbinton in 1969, which had an influence on the inclusion of jazz in local public-school curricula. See Berry, Foose, and Jones 1986, 156.

58. Marquis 2010, 21–29.

59. Ibid.

60. Erskine 1979, 31.

3. NEW ORLEANS EXPOSED TO THE WORLD: THE 1980S

1. "1985," *Times-Picayune*, December 29, 2011, A-7. Garvey and Widmer (2013, 250) note that the record 502 offshore oil rigs in 1981 dropped to 92 by 1986, attributing the decline in oil prices to OPEC.

2. "1984,"*Times-Picayune*, December 28, 2011, A-5. See also Garvey and Widmer 2013, 254.

3. Levin 1985, 38.

4. Marquis 1986–87, 2,

5. See, for example, the reports by Ed Morgan (1984, 19–20); Marquis (1984, 12); and Arlt (1985, 4–6).

6. Arlt 1985, 6.

7. For example, Marquis (1984, 2): "To get to the real point of this Editorial, there is no widespread depression that affects New Orleanians simply because 99 percent of them don't give a damn. If the City of Jazz would have to rely on its local citizens for support, there is a good chance that there would be no jazz, or at best, only private and small get-togethers." This was not the editor's first such observation.

8. Articles in *The Second Line* by eyewitnesses such as Helen Arlt, Pat Wynn, Kelley Edmiston Richards, and Tutone Lyles Naranjo were primary sources in preparing this section of the chapter. (Their focus, however, was on the trad jazz venues.) My sincere thanks go out to all of them for their thorough and conscientious efforts. Note also that Spedale (1984, 271–76) gives an interesting listing of jazz/music clubs and their performing artists as of (presumably) the early 1980s.

9. Naranjo (1989, 22–24): "In the past decade the Sunday jazz brunch has become an increasingly popular New Orleans pastime. Locals and out-of-towners alike enjoy the century-old tradition which combines socializing while being serenaded to the tune of jazz music. Commander's Palace was one of the first restaurants to reinstate this age-old custom so unique to New Orleans. Musical formats vary from a one piece strolling guitarist, to three-piece trios, to sit-down-sextets." The latter would include, for example, the six-piece units put together by longtime musical brunch bassist Joe Simon at Commander's.

10. As I was writing this, I was amused to read a little article in the April 19, 2012, issue of *Forbes Travel Guide*: "Jazz Clubs Are the Newest Trend for Luxe Hotels." Hot news! Among the venues listed was the Davenport Lounge in New Orleans's Ritz-Carlton Hotel—an obvious reference to the weekend gig led by trumpeter Jeremy Davenport. That, like Tim Laughlin's gigs in the lobby bar or Polo Lounge of the Windsor Court Hotel, is one of those that started during the present millennium. But the article seems to miss the point that jazz in fine hotels has quite a long history in New Orleans.

11. Already in the early '80s, Marquis (1983, 2) could note that, "in the twenty-one years I have lived here, the basic roster of musicians playing at Preservation Hall has already dwindled from nearly 200 to roughly twenty-five." This is a trend that would obviously continue for years to come and ultimately lead to a rather dramatic transformation of the venue's original idea.

12. See Jacobsen (2011: 22–23) for this and the following quotations on Bayard's days as a club owner. The one salutary result has been that the experience served as a launching pad for one of the city's most popular and best known bands for the next couple of decades, Banu Gibson's New Orleans Hot Jazz.

13. For more on the opening of the Palm Court, see Marquis (spring 1989, 21–22) and Bookhardt (1989). At the time of this writing, Don Marquis was in the process of prepar-

ing an illustrated history of the Palm Court—hopefully to be published soon. It should be noted as well that George Buck, eighty-three, turned over the management of his business and the GHB Foundation in 2011 to wife Nina, with the day-to-day help of musicians Lars Edegran and Jamie Wight (both of whom frequently play in the club downstairs).

14. Jason Patterson has been the owner of the building at 626 Frenchmen Street since 1975, and he has been my primary source about the history of the clubs in that building since that time. He has also served as musical director at Snug Harbor for most of its history to date. A short-lived club-restaurant featuring folk music—Valentine's—occupied the space from 1977 until 1980, when it came under new management and became known as Faubourg.

15. Wyckoff 1989, N-15. Patterson agrees with that to a degree, saying there is not that much of a local following for modern jazz. But he adds, "Unless you have a mix of tourists and locals, you cannot be a successful jazz club."

16. It became Stafford Tile and Stone Co. Other clubs of the same name have existed in the city. One was located in or near Audubon Park and is said to have flourished in the 1930s. Another, located at 3841 Orleans Avenue in Mid-City, closed as a result of Hurricane Katrina.

17. Brown 2010 (November 8), 28. I am most grateful to Mr. Laredo for sharing this and other information about Tyler's with me in April 2012. I am also grateful to Steve Masakowski for his recollections of Tyler's, which he called "*the* place" for modern jazz in the city after the demise of Lu & Charlie's. He played duets with Marsalis there a couple nights a week in the mid-to-late '80s. Masakowski said that Laredo recorded many of the performances on reel-to-reel tape, but never made them public. "I hope he still has those tapes," he added. He emphasized the importance of Laredo as a supporter of modern jazz in the city who has not been duly recognized. "I think he feels like he's being left out of history," he says.

18. In the late '80s certain neighbors raised a fuss about noise from the club. Litigation relating to its entertainment license resulted, and the venue closed soon thereafter.

19. Jacobsen 2004, 8–9.

20. McCaffrey 2005, 153.

21. McDermott 1993, 33–34. That article was written at a time when racial feelings seem to have been running unusually high in the jazz world, both in New Orleans and nationally. (See also chapter 4.) An account that totally misses/avoids the point of the incident appeared in the *Times-Picayune*, Friday, April 24, 1992, L-20.

22. Davis 1989, B-8.

23. For my brief interview with Sandra Dartus just prior to her retirement and the third installment of Satchmo SummerFest, see Jacobsen 2003, 21–22.

Beginning with the 2013 event, the FQF will be known as "French Quarter Festival Presented by Chevron." The addition of the corporate sponsorship by the petroleum giant is part of a recent trend seen at JazzFest (Shell Oil) and the Superdome (Mercedes-Benz), and beyond. I have mixed feelings about the phenomenon. While I recognize the desperate need for funding to maintain quality, why do these corporate benefactors require that their names be attached to the names of their recipients? Are they paying 100 percent of the bills? They need not be anonymous benefactors, but their "generosity" could be recognized more subtly. Unfortunately, this is the way that corporate sponsorships work throughout this country today.

24. Brown 2011, 8.

25. Mullener 1988, B-1.

26. Brodowski 1989, 33.

27. Brown 2010 (November 8), 55.

28. Jacobsen 2011, 53–65.

29. Brown 2010 (November 8), 64–65.

30. Mullener 1988.

31. Brown 2010 (November 7), 16.

32. Battiste 2010, 166.

33. I interviewed John Mahoney in March 2012, and thank him greatly for the detailed and very useful information he provided about the Loyola jazz program.

34. I spoke to Kidd Jordan by telephone in April 2012. He was ill at the time, and I appreciate very much his taking the time to answer my questions.

35. Kennedy 2002, 90.

36. Burns 2006: 72ff.; Lichtenstein and Dankner 1993: 238–39.

37. Burns 2006: 107–22; Lichtenstein and Dankner 1993, 239–40.

38. Mazza 2003, 50–51. The venue seems to have closed in the 1990s, never again to reopen.

39. A notoriously unpunctual night owl, Ruffins in his "old age" (forty-six), recently changed the starting time for his gigs at Vaughan's from 10 p.m. to 7 p.m. He says the late start caused him to sleep too late on the following day and miss valuable time with his family.

40. Marquis 1989 (winter), 2.

41. Lichtenstein and Dankner 1993, 240; emphasis added.

42. For more about Bayard and the NOCJO, see Jacobsen 2011, 23–25.

43. Fumar 1988.

44. A popular account of the discovery was published early on by Bruce Eggler (1988, B-1–2).

45. E.g. Brothers 2006, 332 n. 98.

46. As of this writing, the latest issue to appear was volume 53, 2003–2009 (spring 2009). But Fred Hatfield has since been named editor. Moreover, he is overseeing the online publication of all issues of the magazine. See www.nojazzclub.org.

47. I wish to thank Danny Gamble, the newspaper's librarian at the time of this writing, for the information based upon research put together by the then–head librarian, Nancy Burris, in 2003. An example of a feature piece on a jazz musician in the *Lagniappe* would be my article about Jack Maheu (Jacobsen 1994).

48. Swenson 2012 (December).

49. Riegel 1988.

50. Gourrier, pers. comm.

51. Burns 2006, 95. This is a quote from a longer Burns interview (95–103) with Brock and reveals a good bit about the man and some of his many contributions to New Orleans music.

52. Adamo 1989, N-3.

53. Giddins 1985, 263–67.

4. A "GOLDEN AGE" FOR TRADITIONAL JAZZ? THE 1990S

1. Van Vorst 2010, 19.

2. *Times-Picayune*, January 6, 2012, A-6.

3. Trumpeter and bandleader Clive Wilson, who plays frequently a both venues, discussed the problem in a 2001 interview (Jacobsen 2011, 188–89).

4. Jacobsen 1994.

5. Jacobsen 2011, 125.

6. Donna and Charlie, a very amiable pair, were back in town in mid-summer 2012. They attended a nostalgic tribute—"Donna's Revisited"—at the Funky Pirate on Bourbon Street, where they were welcomed "home" by Leroy Jones and his band. She told me that she would be retiring from teaching in the Orlando area, where she was named 2013 Teacher of the Year. I wouldn't be surprised if they return to New Orleans—and even get involved in the club scene once again.

7. Ramsey 2012, 8. As it happens, it looks as if the Funky Butt will in fact open once again—but not on North Rampart Street. As of this writing, it is slated to become part of the lively and growing cultural district on Freret Street (Uptown).

8. Wyckoff 2002, 42.

9. Support for the Nickel-A-Dance series has been provided largely by private donors as well as the New Orleans Jazz Celebration (*née* the New Orleans Jazz Centennial Celebration). The NOJC was founded in 1994 and supports a variety of other local series as well, e.g., Jazz at the Sandbar (at UNO) and the Satchmo Club Strut (part of Satchmo SummerFest). Onetime LJF member Jason Patterson is executive director, and its board also includes a number of former members of the Louisiana Jazz Federation.

The co-existence, for a time, of the NOJC, Louisiana Jazz Federation, and the Louisiana Music Commission is a good example—in my opinion—of multiple organizations purporting to do many of the same things.

10. Wyckoff 2002, 43.

11. McCaffrey 2005, 184.

12. Goldman, pers. comm., December 11, 2012.

13. McCaffrey 2005, 277.

14. Jacobsen 1995, 30.

15. Cheatham 1996, 86. I reviewed the book for the *Times-Picayune,* August 18, 1996, E-7.

16. Ibid., 85–86.

17. Ibid., 80.

18. Jacobsen 1997, 42–43.

19. You can read more about his life up to 1997 in my liner notes to his *Echoes of Sidney Bechet* album (Good Time Jazz GTJCD 150006–2, 1997). I highly recommend the music in that fine album as well.

20. The city celebrated the centennial of Jackson's birth in October 2011. As part of the celebration, Dr. Michael White put together an excellent program—"The New Orleans Roots of Mahalia Jackson"—on October 24, 2011, at Xavier University. Calling her "probably the most famous woman to come out of New Orleans," White pointed out her jazz roots, suggesting that she had heard Oliver, Armstrong, and Ory before leaving the city and was influenced by the likes of Bessie Smith and Ma Rainey.

21. Andrea is married to Dr. Gorst DuPlessis, a radiologist and artist, and they have two grown children. It is of interest to me, incidentally, that the majority of people mentioned in the previous paragraph are not native New Orleanians.

22. Much of the following account is based upon an unpublished interview that I conducted with Mrs. DuPlessis in August 1999.

23. DuPlessis, pers. comm., March 2013. George Hocutt first spent time in New Orleans while in the Navy during World War II. After the war he returned to St. Louis, where he got into the record business. He and his wife then moved to California, where he continued in that business. They bought a home in the French Quarter in 1992 and split time between New Orleans and California. While in New Orleans, in addition to co-producing the present CD, he recorded (on the Good Time Jazz label) Chris Tyle's Silver Leaf Jazz Band three times: *Streets and Scenes of New Orleans* (1993); *Jelly's Best Jam* (1993); and *Great Composers of New Orleans* (1996). He also produced Scott Black's *Hot Horns* (Good Time Jazz, 1993), Jacques Gauthé's *Echoes of Sidney Bechet* (Good Time Jazz, 1997) and Duke Heitger's *Rhythm Is Our Business* (Fantasy, 1998). In 2001, he says, "the problems of absentee ownership became more than we wanted to cope with." So they sold their house in the Quarter and somewhat reluctantly moved back to California to live full-time.

24. *The Brooklyn Four Plus One,* Progressive PCD-7109. It was recorded in February 1999, co-produced by Andrea and Wade Barnes.

25. Wade Barnes passed away on March 3, 2012. He was fifty-seven. Andrea DuPlessis produced two other recordings with Barnes and the Brooklyn Repertory Ensemble: *Passport to Brooklyn* (2002) and *Pragmatic Optimism* (2006).

26. Jacobsen 2011, 57.

27. Boeddinghaus's comments are from a detailed (but as yet unpublished) interview that I did with him in June 1994. Incidentally, for other comments about the band and

its philosophy, see my interviews with Duke Heitger and Tom Fischer (Jacobsen 2011, 152–76).

28. These comments are from an unpublished interview that I did with Taylor in December 1995.

29. Clarinetist and bandleader Dr. Michael White has defined Dixieland in the following way (from an interview with Fred Kasten on WWNO radio, July 7, 1994): "In my mind, Dixieland jazz is a watered-down imitation of New Orleans jazz that lacks both musical and spiritual characteristics that make New Orleans jazz have a very distinctive sound. Dixieland is more of a commercial form. Many times, it's played faster and louder than New Orleans jazz, which was originally meant as dance music in many cases. I generally associate New Orleans jazz as being the music that developed from the black musicians in New Orleans, and the initial 'Dixieland' as that being developed by white musicians in imitation of blacks. But the sound and the feeling and spirit were just different." I would agree with that definition, broadly, but his characterization seems to fit best the music of the '40s and '50s, when its chief competitor was bebop.

30. Mayfield 2011, 22–24.

31. See my October 2000 interview with Vappie in Jacobsen 2011, 27–40.

32. Moore's comments are from an interview with the author conducted on May 23, 2012.

33. Pers. comm., March 10, 2013.

34. On "funerals with music," as he calls them, see Stewart 2004. Many of the veteran New Orleans musicians who passed away during this decade, whatever their religious beliefs, were recognized with such funerals. The musical component of the funerals could vary, however. Danny Barker (who died in 1995) did not want such a funeral, but his daughter Sylvia persuaded his wife, Blue Lu, to have one (Jacobsen 2011, 91–94). It turned out to be an impressive occasion, which drew a huge crowd of gawking onlookers. As Stewart (and others) have observed, these farewells sometimes turned into disrespectful "circuses" because of these outsiders.

35. Jacobsen 2011, 57–58.

36. Jordan, in a public speech, April 30, 2013, at an International Jazz Day ceremony honoring him as a "Jazz Hero" by the Jazz Journalists Association.

37. Swenson 2012 (July). For the role of school-based marching bands in the creation of the neo–brass bands, see, for example Roger Hahn (2012) in connection with the Soul Rebels band.

38. Wyckoff 2012, 22.

39. Kimball 1996.

40. John Leo, "The Hazards of Telling the Truth," *Wall Street Journal*, April 15, 2008.

41. Taylor 1994. Another, perhaps more balanced, critic of Marsalis was Gene Lees, whose book *Cats of Any Color: Jazz Black and White* was published just months before the Great Debate. (See my review of the book in the *Times-Picayune*, December 11, 1994.)

42. Jones 1995.

43. And books on the subject keep coming. See, for example, trumpeter Randall Sandke's *Where the Dark and the Light Folks Meet: Race and the Mythology, Politics, and Business of Jazz* (2010).

44. Holley 2012.

5. EPILOGUE: SOME FINAL THOUGHTS

1. National Endowment for the Arts, Office of Research & Analysis, *Survey of Public Participation in the Arts*, June 2009, table 2a.

2. I thank Thiele and Goode for sharing their impressions. Both said that they would be looking to secure more statistically valid information in the future.

3. Jacobsen 2011, 207.

4. See also their website, www.neworleansmusiciansclinic.org.

5. Hurricanes Katrina and Rita brought many hardships to musicians in the city. Accordingly, the New Orleans Musicians Assistance Foundation (NOMAF) was created as an offshoot of NOMC. It, too, has provided much help to musicians at a critical time.

6. This same musician kindly drew my attention to an article on the subject written by jazz journalist Nate Chinen (2008).

BIBLIOGRAPHY

Adamo, Ralph. "New Orleans: Growing Musical Wings." *Billboard*, March 4, 1989, N-3, N-10.

"Alvin Batiste, Sr., Legendary Pioneer of Jazz." Obituary from funeral service held at Gallier Hall, New Orleans, May 12, 2007. Unpublished.

Arlt, Helen. "Third Line." *The Second Line* 35 (Spring 1983): 36–37.

———. "The Third Line." *The Second Line* 37 (Winter 1985): 4–6.

Baker, David N., ed. *New Perspectives on Jazz*. Washington, D.C.: Smithsonian Institution Press, 1990.

Battiste, Harold, Jr., with Karen Celestan. *Unfinished Blues: Memories of a New Orleans Music Man*. New Orleans: The Historic New Orleans Collection, 2010.

Berry, Jason. "Tyler's Fate not an Open and Shut Case." *New Orleans Times-Picayune*, January 22, 1989.

Berry, Jason, Jonathan Foose, and Tad Jones. *Up from the Cradle of Jazz: New Orleans Music since World War II*. 1986. New ed., Lafayette: University of Louisiana at Lafayette Press, 2009.

Bookhardt, Eric. "The Palm Court Café: A Jazz Oasis on Decatur Street." *Wavelength* 5 (January 1989).

Brinkman, Shannon, and Eve Abrams. *Preservation Hall*. Baton Rouge: Louisiana State University Press, 2011.

Brodowski, Pawel. "Coolin' It with Wynton Marsalis." *Jazz Forum* 121 (June 1989): 30–35, 57.

Brothers, Thomas. *Louis Armstrong's New Orleans*. New York: Norton, 2006.

Brown, Anthony. "JASON MARSALIS, NEA Jazz Master (2011)." *Smithsonian NEA Jazz Oral History Interview*, November 7, 2010, www.smithsonianjazz.org.

———. "ELLIS MARSALIS, NEA Jazz Master (2011)." *Smithsonian NEA Jazz Oral History Interview*, November 8, 2010, www.smithsonianjazz.org.

———. "DELFEAYO MARSALIS, NEA Jazz Master (2011)." *Smithsonian NEA Jazz Oral History Interview*, January 13, 2011, www.smithsonianjazz.org.

Burns, Mick. *Keeping the Beat on the Street: The New Orleans Brass Band Renaissance.* Baton Rouge: Louisiana State University Press, 2006.

———, ed. *Walking with Legends: Barry Martyn's New Orleans Jazz Odyssey.* Baton Rouge: Louisiana State University Press, 2007.

Carter, William. *Preservation Hall: Music from the Heart.* New York: Norton, 1991.

Chamberlain, Charles. "Sharing the Stage: Interracial Jazz and Civil Rights in New Orleans, 1946–1970." Public lecture at the Cabildo, New Orleans, April 18, 2008.

Charters, Samuel. *New Orleans: Playing a Jazz Chorus.* New York: Marion Boyars, 2006.

Cheatham, Adophus "Doc." *I Guess I'll Get the Papers and Go Home: The Life of Doc Cheatham.* Ed. Alyn Shipton. London: Cassell, 1996.

Chinen, Nate. "Jazz World Confronting Health Care Concerns." *New York Times,* February 21, 2008 (Music).

Claxton, William, and Joachim E. Berendt. "New Orleans, 1960." *JazzTimes,* December 2005, 44–53.

Darnell, Owen (Duke). "Chicago in New Orleans." *The Second Line* 28 (Winter 1976): 3–5.

———. "Connie Jones: Master Jazzman." *The Second Line* 30 (Summer 1978): 3–9.

Davis, Quint. "Shedding Some Light on the Annual Jazz Festival." *New Orleans Times-Picayune,* March 24, 1989, B-8.

Eggler, Bruce. "Louis: Give or Take a Year." *New Orleans Times-Picayune,* September 24, 1988, B-1–2.

Erskine, Gilbert M. "Further Discussions on Donald M. Marquis' *In Search of Buddy Bolden.*" *The Second Line* 32 (Spring 1979): 29–31.

Feather, Leonard. *Encyclopedia of Jazz.* New York: Bonanza Books, 1960.

———. *Encyclopedia of Jazz in the Sixties.* New York: Bonanza Books, 1966.

———. "New Orleans Awaits Satchmo Statue." *The Second Line* 28 (Spring 1976): 19–21.

Feather, Leonard, and Ira Gitler. *Encyclopedia of Jazz in the Seventies.* New York: Horizon Press, 1976.

Fumar, Vincent. "Banu Gibson Hot on Trail of New Orleans Jazz." *New Orleans Times-Picayune,* December 16, 1988.

Garvey, Joan B., and Mary Lou Widmer. *Beautiful Crescent: A History of New Orleans.* Gretna, La.: Pelican Publishing Co., 2013.

Giddins, Gary. *Rhythm-a-ning: Jazz Tradition and Innovation in the '80s.* New York: Oxford University Press, 1985.

———. "Armstrongland." *Village Voice*, April 15, 1997, 64.

Hahn, Roger. "The Soul Rebels Talk Back." *OffBeat*, January 2012, 65–66.

Hasse, John Edward, ed. *Jazz: The First Century*. William Morrow, 2000.

Herzig, Monika. *David Baker: A Legacy in Music*. Bloomington: Indiana University Press, 2011.

Holley, Eugene, Jr. Interview: "Wynton Marsalis: Jazz Messenger." *Ebony Magazine*, September 2012.

Jacobsen, Thomas W. "Jazz in Greece." *IAJRC Journal* 26, no. 4 (1987): 13–16.

———. "Transplanted Clarinetist Now Local Mentor." *New Orleans Times-Picayune (Lagniappe)*, April 23, 1994, E 1, 10.

———. "Riffs on Racism." *New Orleans Times Picayune*, December 11, 1994, E6–7.

———. "First-Class Celebration." *The Mississippi Rag*, October 1995, 28–30.

———. "New Orleans Notes." *The Mississippi Rag*, June 1997, 42–43.

———. "New Orleans Notes." *The Mississippi Rag*, August 2001, 35.

———. "Jazz in Cuba." *Jazz Notes* (Journal of the Jazz Journalists Association), vol. 13, no. 1 (2002): 24–26.

———. Review of Charles Suhor, *Jazz in New Orleans: The Postwar Years through 1970*. *The Mississippi Rag*, January 2002, 18.

———. "New Orleans Notes." *The Mississippi Rag*, July 2003, 21–22.

———. "Helen Arlt." *Gulfposten*, June–September 2004, 8–9.

———. "Birth of the 'Jazz Church,' Narvin Kimball: *In Memoriam*." *Gulfposten*, Summer 2006, 6.

———. *Traditional New Orleans Jazz: Conversations with the Men Who Make the Music*. Baton Rouge: Louisiana State University Press, 2011.

Jacobsen, Tom, and Don Marquis. "Danny's Boys Grow Up: Part I." *The Mississippi Rag*, May 2006, 1–11.

———. "Danny's Boys Grow Up: Part II." *The Mississippi Rag*, June 2006, 25–32.

Jones, James T., IV. "Racism & Jazz, Same as It Ever Was . . . or Worse?" *Jazz Times*, March 1995, 52–61.

Kennedy, Al. *Chord Changes on the Chalkboard*. Studies in Jazz, No. 41. Lanham, Md.: Scarecrow Press, 2002.

Kimball, Roger. "Greece for the Greeks: History Is Not Bunk." *Wall Street Journal*, February 14, 1996.

Kolb, Carolyn. "Bunny Ears and Cool Jazz: Fifty Years Ago the Playboy Club opened in the French Quarter." *New Orleans Magazine*, March 2012, 60–61.

Laborde, Peggy Scott. *Bourbon Street: The Neon Strip*. 1993. Available on DVD from WYES-TV.

Lasocki, David. *A Higher Fusion: The New Orleans Modern-Jazz Group Astral Proj-*

ect at 34. Astral Project Series, no. 1. Portland, Ore.: Instant Harmony Music, 2012.

Lees, Gene. *Cats of Any Color: Jazz Black and White*. New York: Oxford University Press, 1994.

Levin, Floyd. "New Orleans—July 4, 1976." *The Second Line* 28 (Fall 1976): 16–19.

———. "A Purist's View of the 1985 New Orleans Jazz and Heritage Festival." *The Second Line* 37 (Summer 1985): 38–41.

Lichtenstein, Grace, and Laura Dankner. *Musical Gumbo: The Music of New Orleans*. New York: Norton, 1993.

Marquis, Donald M. *Finding Buddy Bolden: The Journal of a Search for the First Man of Jazz*. Goshen, Ind.: Pinchpenny Press, Goshen College, 1978.

———. "Editor's Comment." *The Second Line* 35 (Summer 1983): 2.

———. "Traditional Jazz at the World's Fair." *The Second Line* 36 (Summer 1984): 13.

———. "Editorial." *The Second Line* 38–39 (Fall 1986–Winter 1987): 2.

———. "George and Nina Buck in New Orleans." *The Second Line* 41 (Spring 1989): 21–22.

———. "Editorial." *The Second Line* 41 (Winter 1989): 2.

———. "A History of New Orleans Jazz, as Told by the Exhibit in the Old U.S. Mint Building." *The Second Line* 47 (1996–97): 4–46.

———. "The New Orleans Jazz Funeral." *The Second Line* 54 (Spring 1999): 11–24.

———. *In Search of Buddy Bolden: First Man of Jazz*. 1978. Rev. ed., Baton Rouge: Louisiana University Press, 2005.

———. "My Life in Jazz." *The Jazz Archivist* 23 (2010): 21–29.

Mayfield, Irvin. *A Love Letter to New Orleans*. New Orleans: Basin Street Records, 2011.

Mazza, Jay. "Getting Loose at the Glass House." *Beat Street*, June 2003, 50–51.

McCaffrey, Kevin, ed. *The Incomplete, Year-by-Year, Selectively Quirky, Prime Facts Edition of the History of the New Orleans Jazz & Heritage Festival*. New Orleans: e/Prime Publications, 2005.

McDermott, Tom. "Skin Game." *Riverfront Times*, March 17, 1993, 33–34.

Miller, Marc. *Louis Armstrong: A Cultural Legacy*. Seattle: University of Washington Press, 1994.

Morgan, Ed. "An Invitation from the 1984 Louisiana World Exposition." *The Second Line* 36 (Winter 1984): 19–20.

Morgan, Thomas L. *Historic Photos of New Orleans Jazz*. Nashville: Turner Publishing, 2009.

Morgenstern, Dan. "History on Record." *Jazz Magazine* 2, no. 1 (1977): 38–44.

Mullener, Elizabeth. "Marsalis Plans Return to Launch UNO Jazz Project." *New Orleans Times-Picayune,* September 29, 1988, B-1–2.

Naranjo, Tutone Lyles. "The New Orleans Jazz Brunch." *The Second Line* 41 (Summer 1989): 22–24.

Newhart, Sally. *The Original Tuxedo Jazz Band: More Than a Century of a New Orleans Icon.* Charleston, S.C.: History Press, 2013.

Piazza, Tom. "Lincoln Center and Its Critics Swing Away." *New York Times,* January 16, 1994, 26H ff.

Raeburn, Bruce Boyd. "New Orleans Style: The Awakening of American Jazz Scholarship and Its Cultural Implications." Ph.D. diss., Tulane University, 1991.

Ramsey, Doug. "They Still Call It JazzFest." www.artsjournal.com/rifftides, November 26, 2011, 1–12.

Ramsey, Jan. "Open the Butt Already." *OffBeat,* November 2012, 8.

Ray, Kathryn Hobgood. "Early Jazz Inspires a Professor, a Band and an Archive." *News from Tulane* (online), October 29, 2012.

Riccardi, Ricky. *What a Wonderful World: The Magic of Louis Armstrong's Later Years.* New York: Pantheon Books, 2011.

Riegel, Stephanie. "Home Town Radio." *Gambit,* December 27, 1988.

Rose, Al, and Edmond Souchon. *New Orleans Jazz: A Family Album.* 3rd ed. Baton Rouge: Louisiana State University Press, 1984.

Saal, Hubert, with Abigail Kuflik. "Jazz Comes Back!" *Newsweek,* August 8, 1977, 50–56.

Sancton, Tom. *Song for My Fathers.* New York: Other Press, 2006, 2010.

———. "Hall that Jazz." *Vanity Fair,* January 2012 (online edition): 1–7.

Sandke, Randall. *Where the Dark and the Light Folks Meet: Race and the Mythology, Politics, and Business of Jazz.* Lanham, Md.: Scarecrow Press, 2010.

Sartisky, Michael, and Thomas A. Dennis, eds. "Musical Notes." *Cultural Vistas,* Winter 1991, 10–12, 26–27.

Smith, Michael P. *New Orleans Jazz Fest: A Pictorial History.* Gretna, La.: Pelican Publishing, 1991.

Smith, Michael P., and Allison Miner. *Jazz Fest Memories.* Gretna, La.: Pelican Publishing, 1997.

Souther, J. Mark. *New Orleans on Parade.* Baton Rouge: Louisiana State University Press, 2006.

Spedale, Rhodes, Jr. *A Guide to Jazz in New Orleans.* New Orleans: Hope Publications, 1984.

Stewart, Jack. *Funerals with Music in New Orleans*. New Orleans: Save Our Cemeteries, Inc., 2004.

Sudhalter, Richard M. *Lost Chords: White Musicians and Their Contribution to Jazz, 1915–1945*. New York: Oxford University Press, 1999.

Suhor, Charles. "Local Jazz Club Secrets Exposed!" *New Orleans Magazine*, February 1975, 72–77.

———. "Jazz in New Orleans in the 1960s." *The Jazz Archivist*, May–December 1995, 1–23.

———. *Jazz in New Orleans: The Postwar Years through 1970*. New Brunswick, N.J.: Institute of Jazz Studies, Rutgers University, 2001.

Swenson, John. "Brass-Pop—Original Pinettes Style." *OffBeat*, July 2012, 36–42.

———. "The Beat Goes On: A 25-Year Retrospective of *OffBeat*." *OffBeat*, December 2012, 35–46.

Taylor, Jeff. "Showdown at Lincoln Center." *I.S.A.M. Newsletter* 24, no. 1 (Fall 1994): 13.

Toyama, Yoshio, and Keiko Toyama. "The Holy Land: New Orleans; The Saint: Louis Armstrong." English translation from Japanese by Hiroshi Owada and Yoshio Toyama. Unpublished, 2008.

VanVorst, Paige. "Chris Tyle." *Jazzbeat* 21, nos. 2–3 (2010): 19–20.

White, Michael G. "Evolution of a Cultural Tradition." *Cultural Vistas*, Winter 1991, 18–21, 36–38.

———. "Dr. Michael White: The Doc Paulin Years (1975–79)." *The Jazz Archivist* 23 (2010): 2–20.

Wood, Brian. *The Song for Me*. 2 vols. Personally published, 2000.

Wood, Harlan. "Bourbon Street—Disjointed." *The Second Line* 28 (Winter 1976): 17–21.

Wyckoff, Geraldine. "Nightspots Unite Musicians, Fans in 'Clubhouse' Community." *Billboard*, March 4, 1989, N-6, N-15.

———. "Frenchmen Desired: Suddenly This Marigny Street Is Sizzling." *New Orleans Magazine*, August 2002, 40–43.

———. "Meet Me at the Second Line." *OffBeat*, September 2012, 22–24.

INDEX

Numbers in italic indicate illustrations.